Smooth Sailing!

AGAINST THE SEA

GREAT ADVENTURE STORIES
— FROM THE PAGES OF —
MOTORBOATING & SAILING

AGAINST THE SEA

GREAT ADVENTURE STORIES
—— FROM THE PAGES OF ——
MOTORBOATING &SAILING

Edited by Louisa Rudeen

AVON BOOKS ◆ NEW YORK

A complete list of permissions can be found on p. 255.

AVON BOOKS, INC.
1350 Avenue of the Americas
New York, New York 10019

Copyright © 1998 by Hearst Communications, Inc.
Front cover photograph courtesy of *Motor Boating & Sailing*
Published by arrangement with *Motor Boating & Sailing*
Visit our website at **http://www.AvonBooks.com**
ISBN: 0-380-79861-1

Library of Congress Cataloging in Publication Data:

Against the sea : great adventure stories from the pages of motor boating &
     sailing / edited by Louisa Rudeen.
          p.   cm.
     Includes bibliographical references.
     1. Boats and boating. 2. Sailing. 3. Motor boating & sailing.
I. Rudeen, Louisa.
GV775.A34   1998   98-22222
797.1'24—dc21   CIP

First Avon Books Trade Paperback Printing: September 1998

AVON TRADEMARK REG. U.S. PAT. OFF. AND IN OTHER COUNTRIES, MARCA REGISTRADA, HECHO
EN U.S.A.

Printed in the U.S.A.

OPM   10 9 8 7 6 5 4 3 2 1

Contents

Preface

"Oh God, Thy ocean is so big, and my boat is so small."

—MARINER'S PRAYER

Motor Boating & Sailing is about boating for pleasure. In the course of working for the magazine, we—*MB&S*'s editors and contributors—have found that most boating is exactly that: a real pleasure. You spend your days cruising on a well-designed, solidly constructed craft in calm waters. On board with you are friends and family, glad for the chance to be spending time together at an unhurried pace. Overhead, seabirds soar through sunny skies. Dolphins leap in your bow wave. You cast out a line and catch your supper. As our Editor-in-Chief and Publisher Peter Janssen writes, "Life doesn't get any better than this."

But this book is not about those carefree times. This is an anthology of adventure stories that have run in the magazine over the past two decades—true stories that deal with those rare occasions when nature turns from a gentle companion to a wrathful enemy; when the going gets rough and there's no place to hide; when it all comes down to a man and woman against the sea.

These stories chronicle the extremes of our sport. Many of them cover natural acts: sudden storms, violent hurricanes, rogue waves, sea creatures that turn deadly. Others are accounts of man-made catastrophes: hijackings, crashes, equipment failures. Some of the tragedies that have stemmed from these disasters at sea may be familiar to you, such as the recent capsizing of a U.S. Coast Guard rescue boat, the sinking of the tall ship *Marques,* and the Fastnet Race that claimed fifteen lives—analyzed here by its winner, Ted Turner.

Another inspiring group of stories in this book paints colorful portraits of men and women who have set off to claim long-distance boating records, including circumnavigating the world—the marine equivalent of climbing Mount Everest. You may have read about some of these adventurers in the newspaper, or seen them on TV. They include Tania Aebi, the youngest woman to sail around the world alone; Dodge Morgan, who broke the nonstop global solo sailing record; and Bryan Peterson, who circumnavigated the globe on an inflatable boat fueled by soybean oil.

Their feats are very much in the tradition of our magazine. Back in 1921, legendary *MB&S* Editor Charles F. Chapman (author of *Chapman Piloting, Seamanship and Small Boat Handling*), sped off with racer Gar Wood to set a record of forty-seven hours and fifteen minutes elapsed running time from Miami to New York in a fifty-foot speedboat. The modern-day seafarers in this book, with their high-tech sailboats or powerboats and navigation equipment, were able to go farther and faster, but they shared the same adventuresome spirit. Through many a dark, howling, waveswept night, they persevered in the face of the vast, unpredictable, and often unmerciful sea.

—Louisa Rudeen
Managing Editor of *Motor Boating & Sailing*

⚓

STAYING ALIVE

After killer whales sink their boat, a couple survives for sixty-six days on a life raft adrift in the Pacific Ocean.

BY SID STAPLETON

The night of Thursday, June 15, 1989 was moonless and overcast. The thirty-eight-foot wooden-hulled cutter *Siboney* was twenty-one days out of Panama, bound for Honolulu. Her master, fifty-nine-year-old Bill Butler, was on a sleepy-eyed watch in the cockpit while his French-born wife Simone, fifty-six, slept soundly below. Winds were out of the south at 12 to 15 knots and the seas were running about six feet—almost perfect sailing conditions for this second leg of the Butlers' planned around-the-world voyage. At 1:30 AM, Bill had logged a satellite-navigation fix which put *Siboney*'s position at 99 degrees, 10 minutes west and 5 degrees, 30 minutes north—some 1,200 miles into the Pacific Ocean off the Central American coast.

At about 3 AM the sea around the boat began to boil with small marine mammals. "They were fairly well scattered and had very large dorsal fins," Bill says. "At first,

I thought they were porpoises. Then I began to see larger animals and realized we had sailed into the midst of a pod of whales. The smaller ones were babies, and the larger ones were cows."

For about an hour, under full mainsail, genoa, and staysail, *Siboney* serenely sailed along with the pod. It was one of those special moments that brings joy to the heart of a deep-ocean sailor. Simone awoke and joined her husband on deck to share the almost magical encounter.

Then their idyllic moment of communing with nature turned into a nightmare. "Much larger animals appeared and began to herd the pod tightly together," Bill says. "Then they began to race in at us. They must have been bulls who saw the boat as some sort of a threat to their cows." In the 35,000 miles of sailing Bill had logged aboard *Siboney*, he had often encountered whales in the open ocean, but these bulls were acting like none he had ever seen. "They were obviously angry," he recalls. "They were not breathing slowly and rhythmically like whales usually do, but were huffing rapidly like runaway locomotives. There were about twenty of them on each side of the boat, shoulder to shoulder. They were black rather than gray, and I distinctly remember their enormous dorsal fins. My best guess is they were killer whales."

The bulls on the port side slammed into *Siboney*'s bow several times, then those to starboard started ramming it broadside. The boat took one especially hard hit on the starboard side and shuddered violently. Simone darted below to check for damage. "Water's coming in!" she shouted. In the few seconds it took Bill to get down to the salon, water was already slopping over its floorboards. The vessel's two bilge pumps had already switched on to fight the deluge. Bill cranked the engine and diverted its raw-water intake so it could help pump the flood back overboard.

Even with three pumps sucking at the torrent, the water had soon risen over his ankles. He fired up the boat's ham radio and broadcast distress calls on two frequencies but got no answer. About five minutes had elapsed since the hit from the whale had opened up one of the boat's seams. Simone looked down at the rising water and said, "I think we'd better get out the life raft."

This was the first voyage on which Bill had ever carried a life raft. With weight and space at a premium, he had selected a four-man Switlik coastal raft as offering the best compromise of cost, size, and weight. *Hell, we'll never need the damned thing anyway,* he had thought when he bought it.

Bill went down into the salon and found the water had risen up over his knees. He tried the radio again; no response. He went topside, inflated and launched the raft, got Simone aboard, and started towing it behind *Siboney.* Then he went back down below to see what else he could salvage. The food locker was already three feet underwater. He dove down and groped in the darkness for whatever came into his hands.

By the time he got back on deck, *Siboney* was almost awash. Less than twenty minutes had elapsed since the shuddering ram by the whale, but he knew she was doomed. It broke his heart to see her foundering. She was a Robert Clark design, built in Southampton, England, in 1938 of Philippine mahogany planking over steam-bent white oak frames. In the twenty-two years he had owned her, Bill had extensively rebuilt her twice—once in 1968 after he had been forced to beach her in the midst of an 80-knot typhoon in the China Sea; again in 1984 when he had covered her with a quarter-inch of epoxy resin and two layers of fiberglass mat, each lapped over the gunwales and carefully secured to the hull with 1,200 brass wood screws.

Sadly he pulled the raft up to *Siboney*'s stern to join Simone. To his horror its rubberized fabric snagged on the cutter's self-steering gear. All the air in one of the two chambers in the raft's single tube whooshed out through the four-inch gash. There was no way to repair the damage until daylight. He climbed in, cut the painter and the raft slipped away from *Siboney*. For the next two hours they floated in darkness with only half of the raft's tube keeping them out of the sea.

At first light, Bill dug out the Switlik's small repair kit and had to use both its patches to seal the cut. After reinflating the raft with its pump, he looked around at the jumble of supplies they had managed to salvage. Simone had grabbed seven or eight tins of canned food and juice, a partial box of cookies, one box of crackers, and a jar of peanut butter. Most important, they had four gallon-and-a-half jugs of water and their Survivor 35, a hand-operated reverse-osmosis watermaker that could produce a liter of fresh water from the sea with about 1,200 strokes of its lever.

On his last trip below, Bill had snatched up his fishing rod, which was rigged with a large hook for catching dolphin (the fish). They also had a Class-B mini Emergency Position Indicating Radio Beacon (EPIRB). He activated it. Surely it would bring help in a few days at most. One of the most treasured possessions aboard the raft was *Siboney*'s logbook. Bill dug out a pencil and decided to make a few entries to chronicle the adventure.

About four o'clock that afternoon, he heaved a sigh of

relief. A huge freighter had risen up on the horizon and was steaming straight for them. Either someone had heard his distress call, or the EPIRB had brought help even sooner than he had dared hope.

They followed the ship's agonizingly slow process until it was within a mile of them, then a half mile, then a quarter of a mile. They began to wave and call out. Mentally they could already see it slow and come to a halt, see its gangplank lower, see the smiling faces of their rescuers beaming down at them.

But something was wrong. The ship was not slowing at all. They waved harder and yelled louder, but the huge vessel kept stubbornly to its inexorable course. It passed within a few hundred feet of them and continued resolutely toward the horizon. As the freighter disappeared into the vastness of the Pacific, they experienced their first bitter taste of the depression that would become one of their greatest enemies.

Bill didn't share all that he knew with Simone. He was an experienced enough seaman to realize their predicament was extremely precarious. Sighting the freighter had been especially astonishing since he had deliberately laid a course well south of the shipping lanes to lessen the danger of a nighttime collision. They also were far off the normal flight paths of any commercial or military aircraft that might receive their EPIRB signal. He felt their best hope was that the signal would be picked up by the COSPASS/SARSAT satellite. What he did not know was that if COSPASS/SARSAT receives an EPIRB signal, the satellite must be in the line of sight of an earth station in order to relay it. From their particular position, such a relay would have been virtually impossible. By the sixth day after *Siboney*'s sinking, the EPIRB's battery was exhausted, and its signal had died.

The sun broiled them by day. At night, a cool ocean breeze chilled them. They had been dressed only in shorts and T-shirts when they abandoned ship and had managed to bring with them only two extra pairs of shorts and T-shirts each.

"The worst part," Bill says, with a shudder in his voice, "was the sharks. We were attacked by thirty to forty of them every day. They didn't attack the raft with their teeth but butted it with their heads. They came at us day and night so that it was almost impossible for us to get any rest, and each one would ram us ten to fifteen times. They would slam into us at bullet speed, then flip over on their backs and spray the raft with urine. They could spray urine eight, ten, fifteen feet in the air. To finish off the attack, they'd give the raft a great slap with their tails. After a couple of weeks of that sort of punishment, you'd really begin to look at the raft's seams and wonder 'How much of this can they take and still hold together?' " About three o'clock one morning, a shark hit the bottom so hard it actually tore a two-inch gash in the floor. Bill found a needle and thread that had mercifully gotten caught up in the supplies they'd put aboard and hastily repaired the damage.

At her home in Westchester, New York, Bill's married daughter Sally Smith was getting concerned. Since the beginning of their voyage, her dad and Simone had checked in via ham radio every two or three days. The last contact had been over a week earlier. Bill had told the family not to worry unless they went three weeks without contact. Even so, Sally called the Coast Guard to see if they had any news of the vessel. The officer at

*the Pacific Operations Center in California told her not to worry.
Under the best of conditions, he said, it would take a sailing
vessel like* Siboney *at least forty-five days to make the passage
from Panama to Honolulu, and it could take as long as sixty
days. Her parents were probably fine; their radio was just on
the blink.*

By day twenty, the food Bill and Simone had salvaged
off *Siboney* was gone. "At that point," he says, "we were
each eating only half a saltine cracker for breakfast, half
a cracker with a little peanut butter for lunch, and half a
cracker again for dinner."

The water around the raft was alive with sea creatures
who found welcome shade in its shadow. Bill had his
fishing rod with its hook, but no bait. After hours of work,
he had straightened the hook and lashed it to the life
raft's tiny oar for use as a harpoon. But the fish were too
fast for him and he had been unable to strike a single
one. He had to have some kind of bait. Sea birds alighted
on the raft almost every day. He wanted to try to catch
one and use its flesh for bait, but Simone protested.
"They're so beautiful, and they're our only company,"
she said weakly. "You can't kill them." With each passing
day, Simone was sinking deeper into despair; Bill couldn't
bring himself to make her more unhappy.

He looked longingly at the turtles that floated by the
raft within easy reach. But they were massive—four feet
across and 50 to 60 pounds each. He was far too weak to
get such a creature into the raft.

They had had nothing to eat for three days when a
small turtle with a shell only about a foot-and-a-half
across swam by within reach. Bill grabbed it, wrestled it
into the raft and slit its throat. "We ate about half of him

for lunch," he says with a chuckle. "It was the best food we had on the entire trip."

With the turtle's flesh for bait, Bill spent several more hours bending his single fishhook back into its original shape and started fishing. "I was trying to catch dolphin," he says, "but the triggerfish would run them off and take the bait themselves. Over the next three to four weeks, I caught four to five hundred pounds of fish. Every day I'd eat about eleven or twelve raw fillets, which equaled about two pounds of meat, and forced Simone to eat two or three fillets. When she became so weak and despondent she didn't want to eat, I told her to think of her family. Finally she'd eat."

Sally Smith was really worried. It had been over five weeks since anyone had heard from her dad and Simone. She was calling the Coast Guard's Pacific Operations Center daily, but they insisted they would launch no search until Siboney *became overdue in Honolulu. That could be another three weeks. A chill ran up her spine when she recalled a book she'd read:* Survive the Savage Sea *by Scotsman Dougal Robinson. On June 15, 1972—seventeen years to the day and while sailing the same route as* Siboney—*the Robinson family's boat had been sunk by a killer whale and they'd spent thirty-eight days adrift in a life raft.*

DAY 36: Land! It was there, well to the south. As the current carried the raft within about five miles of it, Simone wanted to swim for it. But Bill knew that even with land that close, in their weakened condition they would never reach it. And he thought about the sharks. "The raft is our home," he told her firmly. "We don't leave it for any reason until we're rescued." The land turned out to be an island (from their track, possibly Cocos Island), which slowly disappeared below the horizon.

As despondent as they were over drifting past the island, they had an even more pressing problem: The fishing had turned bad. Bill had risked his last scrap of bait, but the fish had taken it without being hooked. They had had nothing to eat for two days. Suddenly the water around them began churning with activity. A porpoise was feeding on a school of small fish below the raft, and they were frantically trying to escape its attacks. One of the small fish leaped high in the air. Bill grabbed it with his hands and pulled it down into the raft. Then another. And another. "I caught four fish by hand within about fifteen minutes," he says. "From that point on, I had no further difficulty catching enough fish to survive."

The weather had evolved into a cycle of two days of raging storms, two days of blinding sun, then two days of storms. The raft's canopy, which had shielded them from the daytime sun and the slashing rain, had lost its waterproofing. After every drenching downpour, they had to bail out the raft. Everything aboard was soaked, and they had to spread their clothes to dry in the sun. Some of the clothes stank so badly and were so rotted that they had to throw them overboard.

DAY 59: Land again! And this was no island. It stretched long and low across the entire eastern horizon. It had to be the coast of Central America. For two days they watched the green hills come closer and closer and were certain they would be swept into shore. But then the land seemed to stop getting any closer. For two days, then three, it hung tauntingly on the horizon. Bill felt a sinking feeling inside as he realized the eastward-flowing current that had carried them almost 1,200 miles toward safety was now curving to the northwest and carrying them parallel to the coast.

Ahead, he could distinguish a point of land jutting well out into the sea. Beyond the point, the coastline fell away sharply. The point was probably their last chance. If they were swept past it, the curving current would carry them away from land and sweep them farther and farther back out into the Pacific. With what little strength he had left, Bill rowed the clumsy raft for hour after hour. He wasn't certain he was making any progress, but he had to try.

It was about four o'clock on the hot, clear afternoon of Saturday, August 19—day sixty-six of the Butlers' Pacific drift. The Costa Rican Coast Guard patrol vessel *Punta Burica* was about five miles offshore conducting a random pattern search for a missing shrimp boat. The helmsman spotted something small and low in the water less than a mile away. He thought it was probably a fishing buoy, but he raised his binoculars to check it out.

"The coast had been in sight for a week, but we couldn't seem to do anything to get the raft closer to it," Bill says. "We were so weak we didn't even hear the patrol boat until it was almost on top of us. The time from the instant we first heard its engines and looked up until they were hoisting us aboard couldn't have been more than two or three minutes."

At the hospital in Golfito, Costa Rica, Bill found his normal 175 pounds had shrunk to 126—a loss of 49 pounds. Simone had lost 58 pounds. They were incredibly weak, but had never lost their mental alertness and were pronounced basically fit by their doctors.

Will they ever go to sea again? "Oh sure," Bill told me the day after their release from the hospital. "We'll be back. But we'll stick to coastal cruising. We'll leave the deep-ocean passages to someone else."

November, 1989

⚓

HIJACKED

Looking down the barrel of a hijacker's gun, the captain and mate of the sportfisherman Rapscallion *figure they are dead men.*

BY MICHAEL VERDON

It seemed like just another routine charter. Larry Withall, captain of the sixty-five-foot Hatteras sportfisherman *Rapscallion,* had made the crossing from Fort Lauderdale to Bimini in the Bahamas three times already that month, and he assumed this trip would be no different from any other fishing charter. Little did he and his mate, Jason "Tiny" Walcott, think they'd soon be victims of a hijacking.

Sure, there were some warning signs. After the client, calling himself "Brian," had come and inspected the vessel, he paid for the charter in cash—$3,000 in twenty-dollar bills. While that seemed unusual to Larry, it wasn't an unheard-of way to pay for a charter. Many of his clients liked to deal on a cash-only basis to keep it off the books. Besides, the charter agent had vouched for Brian, saying he was the son of a wealthy Chilean factory owner.

"He really looked the part," says Larry. "A rich South American all the way. Ralph Lauren jeans, Tommy Hilfiger shirt, Timberland shoes—all name-brand labels. He was a real fast talker, real smooth."

The men shook hands and agreed to meet Friday morning. But Brian—with another man called "Jose"—didn't show up until Saturday afternoon. Larry was concerned; he'd wanted to leave early and now they wouldn't get to Bimini before dark.

Throttling up *Rapscallion*, Brian headed out into the Atlantic at 30 knots. The Gulf Stream crossing was uneventful; Larry and Tiny monitored the electronic instruments, while Brian sat and chatted. "He seemed like a nice guy," Larry says.

When *Rapscallion* reached its destination, the "nice guy" turned into a psychopath. "As I was lining up the markers into Bimini," says Larry, "Jose came up to the bridge and asked Tiny to get him some aspirin."

The mate went below, only to find Brian pointing a machine gun at him. "Get on the ground!" Brian screamed. "Or I'll blow your head off! We're stealing your boat!"

As he lay on the cabin sole, Tiny could feel the gun being pressed against the back of his head. He could also feel shackles being locked around his ankles and his hands being cuffed behind his back. "If you give us any trouble," said Brian, "I'll cut your guts out and throw you overboard."

He explained that they were heading for the southern Bahamas, where they would rendezvous with another vessel to refuel. "If you cooperate," Brian said to Tiny, "we'll let you go. We won't hurt you."

Judging from Brian's erratic behavior, Tiny didn't hold

much faith in that promise. Neither did Larry—after the hijacker came up on the flying bridge and leveled the gun at his chest. "I turned around and saw him with the gun," says Larry. "I thought he was joking and said, 'Did my mate put you up to this?' " In reply, Brian threw a pair of handcuffs at him. "Put them on," he said.

Within minutes, Larry was cuffed to the steering wheel and the boat was headed south—away from Bimini. Brian wanted to make an offshore run for the southern Bahamas, but Larry convinced him that passing between Cat Cay and Gun Cays would save time and fuel. During the next hour, Brian resumed his nice-guy demeanor, speaking freely. He had a client "down south," he told Larry, "who wants this boat. No questions asked."

Larry was now convinced he'd been set up, but he was not sure by whom. "He knew way too much about me," he says. "My mom's name and address, where my girlfriend lived, even the name of my bank where I got a homeowner's loan."

As they navigated the shallow waters between Gun and Cat cays, Larry grew concerned about Tiny. He asked Brian if he could see his mate. "No way," Brian replied, but did offer to bring back a note. While the hijacker was below, Larry heard screaming. When Brian returned with no note and a silencer on his gun, Larry assumed the worst. He knew then that the only way he could get off *Rapscallion* was by his own resources. His captor confirmed it when he said, "You're such a nice guy. It's a pity I have to kill you."

Larry figured he had one chance. "I told him I needed to go up on the tower to navigate," he says. "It was pitch-black and the cut is filled with reefs, so that made sense. But I didn't think he'd go for it."

To Larry's surprise, Brian replied, "No problem." Unshackled, Larry climbed up the sportfisherman's tuna tower and began to steer from up there. Brian, reading numbers from the depthsounder on the flying bridge below, remained out of view. Larry heard his voice, calling out, "Ten feet, eight feet, twelve feet."

Plucking up his courage, Larry pushed the throttle forward, turned the wheel hard over, and jumped. "I expected to feel bullets hitting the water when I came up for air," he says. But all he heard was a voice, growing ever fainter, calling, "Twelve feet, eight feet, nine. . . ."

Less than a minute later, *Rapscallion* was hard aground. Brian, frantic with panic and rage, raced down to the cabin and pulled Tiny, who was alive and unharmed, out of the chair. "Your captain's jumped," Brian shouted in his face. "You have to get us out of here. *Now!*" The hijacker took off Tiny's handcuffs and marched him up to the flying bridge. "He put the gun in my ear and screamed at me to get going," Tiny says. Able to start only the port engine, he backed the boat off the reef.

In the meantime, Larry was being carried away from shore by an outgoing tide. To his horror, he saw *Rapscallion* turn and start to bear down on him. "I was a half mile from shore and saw the boat come straight at me," he says, "and I really didn't think I was going to make it."

Fortunately, another shoal lay between the boat and its captain. *Rapscallion* hit hard a second time and keeled over to starboard, leaving the port propeller—the one that still worked—sticking way out of the water. Black smoke started pouring from the exhaust and the engine went dead.

"The guy really freaked out on me then," Tiny says.

"He kept telling me that my life depended on getting the engines going."

But the diesels wouldn't even kick over. *Rapscallion* wasn't going anywhere. "The gun was pointed at me," says Tiny. "But I could see he was looking at his handheld GPS. I figured I had to try something or it was over."

Mustering up all his strength, the mate ran at the hijacker and punched him in the head. "I could feel the bullet go by my left ear," says Tiny, who wrestled his captor to the deck. "I heard four more shots go off. I figured I was hit, but I kept fighting."

Brian recovered himself and put the gun against Tiny's head. "I should kill you now," he told the mate, handcuffing him to a rail, "but I will let you drown instead." Believing that *Rapscallion* was sinking, the two hijackers got into the life raft and floated away with the current. The sixty-five-foot Hatteras keeled over so far that, to Tiny, it seemed like his captors might be right: He would drown, chained to the flying-bridge rail.

Larry, in the meantime, had been swimming for his life. Stung by jellyfish and near exhaustion, he finally staggered ashore an hour and a half later on Cat Cay. In only his boxers, he made his way to the local police station. The wide-eyed Bahamian constables didn't know what to make of him as he hysterically told his story and requested aid for his mate. When nobody helped him, Larry called the U.S. Coast Guard. They were on the scene in less than half an hour. He met the pilot of a Coast Guard helicopter who assured him that Tiny was fine, and had been taken to Bimini. The pilot told Larry that he would refuel the chopper and come back for him. He never returned.

Instead, as Larry was sitting in the police station, he heard a vehicle pull up outside. Looking through the Venetian blinds, Larry was horrified to see the two hijackers sitting in the backseat of a golf cart.

"The local manager of a resort had found them," he says. The hijackers had a very different story than the one Larry was telling the local Bahamian officials. "They'd said they had come across the Gulf Stream in a small center console and it had flipped over," says Larry.

Not knowing whom to believe, the officials decided to arrest all three men and put them in the same cell. During the night, the two hijackers made repeated threats to kill Larry. "We were being guarded by a kid with an M-16," says Larry. "He was listening to rap music at full volume, so he wasn't paying attention. I could hear the two guys trying to break free, so I kept yelling at him to turn the music down. He'd turn it down, look at them and then turn it up again. It was the longest twenty-four hours of my life."

The next morning, Larry was brought to Bimini, where he met Tiny. The mate, after being dropped off by the Coast Guard, had also been arrested and sent to jail in chains. After confirming their identities, they were released.

When Larry returned to *Rapscallion*, he found the boat stripped clean. "Everything that wasn't bolted down was gone," says Larry. "All my tools and fishing tackle—about $70,000 worth of equipment."

But the police did find some documents that created a paper trail to where the hijackers probably had been headed. They included U.S. Customs papers for export with the boat's name filled in, a phony bill of sale, cruising guides to the Caribbean, and a Colombian courtesy flag.

Three days after it was grounded, *Rapscallion* was backed off the rocks and brought back to Fort Lauderdale. The pair of hijackers were tried in the Bahamas for kidnapping and attempted murder, and sentenced to jail time. After their return to Florida, Larry and Tiny continued to lead charters to the Bahamas on other boats. But that night on *Rapscallion* was a trip they will never forget.

April, 1996

⚓ FASTNET DISASTER

The toll is fifteen dead in yacht racing's blackest night. The winner tells what went wrong—and how he survived.

BY TED TURNER

It was the roughest race I've ever been in. It was the roughest race in the history of offshore racing. I've sailed over 100,000 miles offshore in some of the toughest races around the world—the Sydney to Hobart, the Rio Circuit, the '72 Bermuda Race, and a number of Transatlantic races—and I've never seen the likes of the conditions encountered in this Fastnet Race, which began in Portsmouth, England, on Saturday, August 11, 1979. It will go down not only in sailing history, but in the history of all sports, as one of the worst disasters ever.

It was big. Everything about it was big. The 306-boat fleet, the 160 boats that retired, the 60-knot winds, the 30- to 40-foot waves, the twenty-three boats that were sunk or abandoned, the 136 people who were rescued, the death toll of fifteen—everything about the race was on a scale never before contemplated.

As we neared Fastnet Rock off the Southeast coast of

Ireland on Monday evening, we got word that something strong was coming. My boat *Tenacious*'s navigator, Peter Bowker, had been monitoring the weather reports and learned that in about six hours we would be hit by winds up to Force 10 (55 knots on the Beaufort Scale).

We rounded the Rock at about 6:30 Monday evening, and from then until the middle of the night the southeasterly wind increased. My America's Cup tactician, Gary Jobson, was watch captain at the time. As the wind came up we threw a reef in the main, and changed down from the No. 2 genoa to the No. 3 headsail. An hour later our main was triple-reefed and we had the No. 4 headsail up. It seemed as if no sooner did we get sail shortened than it was time to strike some more. Although *Tenacious* is big (sixty-one feet), you have to be careful not to let her get overpowered. It always pays to get sail off her quickly when it breezes up.

Around midnight when I came on deck it was blowing about 35 knots and we were making 8½ to 9 knots of speed down the rhumb line, hard on the wind. Then, in a short period of time, maybe twenty to thirty minutes, the storm hit us with winds rising to 60 knots.

It was pitch black. You couldn't see anything. The sea spray was like bullets. Our deck lights had gone out except for our emergency running lights. The crew was huddled on the windward deck with their backs to the full brunt of the storm. They were sitting there like statues, their harnesses secured to the deck. The sea had come up as fast as the wind. It was getting rough.

I remember saying to the crew that twenty men would die that night. Regretfully, those turned out to be prophetic words. All told, as far as I know, twenty-one people died that night in the Irish Sea—fifteen in the race, four aboard a capsized multihull, and two aboard a cruising boat near the Scilly Isles.

It was obvious I had to tell my men to strike the mainsail. We had waited far too long to take it in and I didn't know how they were going to do it. Slowly, five men crawled to the mast and along the boom, hooked on their harnesses, and went to work. The wind was howling so loud that you could hardly hear the man shouting next to you. Everything had to be yelled twice.

Slowly, carefully, the crew wrestled with the wildly flapping main, taking in a bit and lashing it to the boom as they went. In twenty minutes the main was fully struck and secure. One of the toughest chores of the night had been accomplished. The crew was superb.

But now an even more dangerous situation developed. I was chilled by the prospect of running down one of the little boats in the fleet. As we were rocketing down the course away from the Rock, we were sailing right through a fleet of over 100 small boats still trying to make their way to it.

The seas had built to twenty feet and the little boats would be hidden in the valleys of these gray-bearded mountains. If we hit one of the lightly constructed fiberglass boats, *Tenacious* would crush it, smash it in two, and everybody aboard would be killed.

Of all the things that happened that night, that was my greatest fear, and that is the only thing that had me scared—that, and the fear that something aboard *Tenacious* might break, causing us to lose the race.

All of a sudden we saw the running lights. They flashed into view and then disappeared behind a wave. Where were they? They were dead ahead. But how far? It was impossible to tell. Even though we were on starboard track and had right-of-way, we bore off, going 90 degrees to the course. Somehow we missed them. Time and again for the next several hours we radically altered course because one of us thought he saw a light ahead.

Tenacious was now barely under control. With just the No. 4 headsail up and thirty-foot seas hitting our windward bow and abeam, we were slewing wildly. With only the small headsail up, the boat was badly out of balance and steering was difficult. The boat responded sluggishly.

When a storm like this comes up fast, the distance between waves is short and that is what made the situation difficult. The waves began building and every now and then a really large one would come along, breaking, cascading tons of water down its side. As I shot a glance to windward I could see that the waves were halfway up the mast height when we were in the troughs. Then we would be hit abeam, a huge breaking sea washing over *Tenacious* and knocking us flat on our side. Again and again we were hit by these seas that knocked us flat—it happened perhaps six or seven times during the night.

It is difficult to adequately describe the conditions in the early hours of Tuesday morning. And I must admit that I've already forgotten a lot of what happened. I've unconsciously wiped a lot of that night from my mind. I think that is a human reaction when things get really catastrophic. It's like childbirth—the mother forgets the pain and what it was really like.

Throughout the night we just hung on and I steered. As time went on the wind clocked around, as we knew it would, so our course to the finish was the shortest one, except for those times we took evasive action to avoid the smaller boats. It was all I could do to steer and watch the sail. I had one of the crew stand next to the binnacle and read off the compass headings as the boat lurched down the course. When a big sea would well up behind us, I bore off and rode it down. In the troughs the wind would abate, then as we rode up to a crest we would be slapped with a blast of 60-knot wind. Later, we put up the storm trysail, a sail designed for heavy conditions, and that helped the balance and control.

It was still dark as we approached the Scilly Isles off the southwest coast of Cornwall, England, off Land's End. This is a real graveyard of lost vessels, ships that came to grief on the rocky shores of this cluster of islands on nights just like this one. These rocks were the next and last big danger of the race. We didn't know how much leeway we were making or how far off course we had gotten because of our evasive action. Since loran and other electronic aids to navigation were prohibited in the race, we were not sure exactly where we were. Nobody was. The only thing you could do was take an RDF (Radio Direction Finder) bearing off the Scillys.

Because the boat was jerking around so violently, Bowker could not get an RDF bearing. So, we decided to play it safe, coming up and giving the Scilly Isles a really wide berth. It was a matter of the safety of the ship and the crew versus winning the race. Bowker repeatedly tried to take RDF bearings, because now the distance sailed was crucial to winning. Finally he maneuvered himself aft to get away from interference from the boom and rigging and stood up—without a harness—to take a bearing. Just then a breaking wave washed over the boat and slammed him to leeward. Only the stern pulpit kept him on deck. If he had been washed overboard, I'd say there would have been less than a fifty-fifty chance of our getting back to him. That's how bad the conditions were. You really couldn't maneuver.

Nor could you go to the aid of another boat with any degree of safety. In fact, many of the boats that came to grief were ones that answered distress flares. By deviating from their course (the best one for small boats in survival conditions), they were forced to take the seas broadside and that is when they got into trouble. During the height of the storm we certainly could not have come to the aid of a vessel in distress without endangering our boat and crew. It is a wonder the small boats even tried.

As time went on, the distance between the waves increased, and as it did everything became more manageable. By the time we had cleared the Scilly Isles, the wind had dropped to 35 knots and we set two headsails, wing-and-wing. Nevertheless, I reckon we lost about an hour by leaving the islands so far to port.

What caused the Fastnet disaster? Although the best and most authoritative answer will come from the inquiry by the British Yacht Racing Association, a few observations seem obvious:

First, there were 306 boats in the race. Whenever you have that many boats you increase your chances of disaster.

Second, the Royal Ocean Racing Club permits very small boats to race in the Fastnet. This year the minimum waterline length was only twenty-one feet. Although the conditions were tough for *Tenacious*, we were never really in a survival situation. Only once did I briefly think of heaving-to. *Tenacious* is strong. That's why I have her. But for the little boats, it was a survival situation. Practically all the boats that had serious problems were under forty feet. The same seas that were knocking the big, heavy *Tenacious* down were rolling over the thirty-three-footers.

Third, the wind came up fast and when it does the seas are always short. The short seas don't give a small boat time to recover—and they also are more apt to be breaking seas. The only time I've been through anything like them was years ago when I was delivering *Bolero* from New York to Florida and we got caught in a gale a few miles off Diamond Shoals.

Fourth, although the water was considered relatively warm for the Irish Sea, in fact a man could only live in it for a few hours before dying of hypothermia. That's how a number of people died who were washed overboard, or who were washed out of life rafts.

Already the critics are saying that the race should have been called off. I disagree. Each skipper could have called the race off for himself whenever he wanted to. In fact, more than half of them did.

The RORC Special Regulations say, among other things, that "the safety of a yacht and her crew is the sole and inescapable responsibility of the owner, who must do his best to insure that the yacht is fully found, thoroughly seaworthy, and manned by an experienced crew who are physically fit to face bad weather."

Good seamanship is what ocean racing is all about. But most people have forgotten that. Most races are in light to moderate conditions, so people don't get the kind of experience they need to face conditions like these. I've raced over 750 days, all told, offshore—and only one or two have been this bad. Tornadoes occur each year, too, but how many houses are tornadoproof?

What really bothers me is that a lot of owners in this race, who should have known better, didn't even carry a

storm trysail, and that includes a number of famous British yachtsmen. The reason was simply to save forty
pounds of weight. Not only did I have a storm trysail
aboard, but I also had a spare mainsail—and despite all
that extra weight I still won the race.

If the owners had followed the spirit as well as the letter
of the RORC racing rules they would have been far better
off. You're supposed to have a strong vessel with crew
and equipment for any condition. I feel a little like Noah.
I knew that the flood was coming, and I had a boat ready
that would get me through it.

It was a storm precisely like this one that saved England
from the Spanish Armada. Whenever you sail in the English Channel, you've got to be prepared for the return of
that storm.

October, 1979

⚓

THE LONGEST RIDE

Two MB&S *editors drive a Tempest 38 speedboat from Miami to Maine—in five days.*

BY PETER A. JANSSEN

We were only a mile or so outside the bridge at Norfolk, Virginia, and with the seas cresting at ten to twelve feet and the wind working its way upward of 35 knots, we were getting pretty badly beaten up. The bow of our thirty-eight-foot Tempest speedboat would climb up one wave and then plunge into the trough on the other side. Up and down, up and down. The waves were too big and too uneven to power across them; it simply was a matter of up one and down the other, for as far as the eye could see.

Then, suddenly, an off-center, out-of-sequence wave caught the boat and hurled it sideways into the trough— like a champion wrestler picking up his opponent and throwing him to the canvas. With a bone-crunching crash the Tempest landed flush on its starboard side, on the topsides, not on the hull. The entire boat shuddered and then slowly righted itself, in time to climb the next wave and bury the bow in the trough, sending tons of cold green water cascading back on top of us.

The two of us, *Motor Boating & Sailing* Contributing Editor Jerry Berton and I, were more than halfway through an epic trip from Miami to Maine on the Tempest, which was powered by twin Evinrude V-8, 275–horsepower outboards. At this point, however, about 5:30 on an early summer Sunday afternoon, we weren't worried about getting to Maine; we were worried about getting to shore.

As we were bashing about, a Coast Guard helicopter hovered almost directly overhead, and a few seconds later a small Coast Guard cutter pulled up twenty or thirty yards away. Over the VHF radio they said they were on a search-and-rescue mission for a boat that had capsized. Had we seen anything? We hadn't. But we were hoping to make it farther north that night, so we asked about conditions up the coast. Turn back, they said, turn back.

Unfortunately, that was easier said than done. Turning back was precisely the problem. As long as we kept the bow into the waves, the boat was under control. Trying to turn around, turning sideways, left us susceptible to a broach. But we had no choice. Masterfully timing the waves and working the throttles, Berton got us around and—pushed by a terrible following sea—we sped back under the bridge and swept toward the nearest shore.

At that moment, this trip didn't seem like one of my better ideas. Several months before, however, it had seemed pretty good. Then, I thought, why not take on the grand tradition of the magazine, tackling long distances and unpredictable offshore weather to see what the best new boats and engines could do. Back in 1921, for example, legendary *MB&S* editor Charles F. Chapman sped off with racer Gar Wood and two others to set a record of forty-seven hours and fifteen minutes elapsed running time from Miami to New York in a fifty-footer. We just wanted to go a little farther—to take on the entire east coast of the United States. It had a nice ring to it; it was an adventure worth doing.

So late in the spring I had lunch with Adam Erdberg, the energetic president of Tempest Marine in North Miami, to lay out the idea. We needed a boat big enough, reliable enough, and fast enough to make it all the way— about 1,800 miles. The idea would be to run about twelve hours a day, to go inside on the Intracoastal Waterway if the weather was rough, or to stay outside in the ocean if we could make time, and to come in at night, wherever we were. We figured that the entire trip would take about five days. We were right about that—in fact, we did make it in five and a half days, setting a record of sorts. We thought it would be a piece of cake. We were wrong about that.

As it turned out, almost everything—short of sinking the boat—happened to us.

Over the years, I'd done parts of the trip, in various boats, with various companions—but never the entire Miami-to-Maine voyage. And Berton had done the Miami-to-New York run in a thirty-two-foot speedboat— but also had never gone all the way up to Maine in the same expedition. We didn't know anybody who had done it in one shot—particularly in an open speedboat. So off we went.

The Tempest is a pretty boat—slim, sleek, sensuous. It's also a serious offshore boat, with a twenty-five-degree deadrise at the transom, ready to cut through rough water. And it's solid as a rock.

Because of the outboards, the boat, a San Remo model,

has an enormous amount of space in the cockpit. The driver and navigator are enclosed in heavily-cushioned bolster seats that drop down; you can either stand or sit, depending on the sea conditions (standing is actually far more comfortable in anything rougher than flat water). Two identical bolster seats lie behind the driver and navigator, and then there's a comfortable, padded U-shaped seat all the way aft. Forward, the cabin has facing settees, a head under a center cushion, and a V-berth all the way up into the bow.

On board we had a new Furuno loran, which Erdberg had just put on for the trip. We also carried on an emergency inflatable raft, hurriedly hustling it below as if to deny its existence—or the possibility that we might need it.

As we loaded up the boat, we were a bit nervous. We were worried about the boat, the engines, ourselves. Had we spent enough time preparing everything? (Probably not.) Was there something we'd overlooked? Would the new loran, bolted on the night before, even work? We had the regular Coast Guard safety package: flares, extra first-aid kit, duct tape, tools. Were they the right ones? Did we have enough oil for the high performance outboards? (No.) Evinrude had told dealers along the way about our trip so they would have spare parts if we needed them quickly. We stored two extra props, screwed down in big boxes, up in the V-berth.

We couldn't figure out our gas consumption or range; the engines had only been run for five hours to break them in. We also weren't sure if the fuel gauge was accurate, so we asked Erdberg about the tanks' capacity. About 195 gallons, he replied. Unfortunately, we were to test this on our own a few days later.

We meant to get under way early in the morning but, as those things go, we finally left the Tempest factory in North Miami just before noon. Loading up the boat, topping off the tanks, making all the last-minute adjustments for a long trip, always seems to take longer than you think.

In any event, we waved good-bye to Erdberg and sped south—the wrong way—down the Intracoastal Waterway (ICW) to Biscayne Bay and Miami with an accompanying photo boat for some pictures, and then finally pulled out into the ocean at Haulover Inlet about 12:30 with a very wary eye on the weather. In Miami itself the day was beautiful, sunny and in the high eighties. But threatening, dark clouds were building up to the west, and the national forecast was showing storms farther north. Not ideal, but then you can't plan an 1,800-mile trip without expecting to get wet.

Running in the ocean, the Tempest quickly settled into an easy stride, warming to the task ahead. With the throttles from 5600 to 5800 rpm, we were running at an easy 45 to 46 miles per hour. The wind was off the starboard quarter and the seas kicked up at times so we were occasionally airborne, but it was the perfect opening for a speedboat journey—an easy, fast ride. Better yet, the engines were humming, not blasting away, so that we could actually talk to each other. We were definitely off to a good start.

After a few hours we pulled in at Fort Pierce for gas. Unsure of our capacity and distrusting the gauge, we wanted to play it safe. After we tied up, we were reminded of what was to be an unpleasant fact of life for the next five days. Under way, it was totally impossible to use the head under the seat cushion in the front of the cabin. In fact, it was also impossible to use it when we were tied up, since we couldn't find the fittings. This meant that, as soon as we tied up, our first question to the dock master had a certain predictability. "Excuse me, but where's the head?" At Fort Pierce he not only pointed in the right direction, but he also told us the combination lock on the door. Needless to say, we both forgot it in our rush to get there. How, we wondered, were we going to navigate to Maine if we couldn't remember four numbers to open the bathroom door?

After this first run, we also became aware of some other facts of life. First, the speedometer didn't work. Second, the compass seemed to swing through about 30 degrees without bothering to settle down anywhere. Third, we still weren't used to the loran, so our entire navigation was somewhat in doubt. Fourth, we weren't sure if the bilge pump worked. Fifth, the starboard engine had a habit of dying when shifted into reverse at idle—a habit that made docking lots of fun, particularly since you weren't exactly sure of when it would conk out. Finally, we figured the boat consumed slightly more than a gallon per mile—and it also took an entire case of oil—twelve quarts—at every fuel stop. This meant opening twelve quarts, pouring them into the two oil tanks in the transom, one by one, wiping up the spills, and hoping that things wouldn't get worse. At first, this process ate up some time, although later on we did get pretty efficient at it.

Since the weather was looking worse, we ran inside from Fort Pierce to Daytona, pulling into the Daytona Boat Works at 7:45, well before dark. We definitely were taking it easy the first day. The sun went down about 8:30, so we could have gone a bit farther, but things were going well and we didn't want to press our luck. In addition, I like Daytona. Before we tied up for the night we filled the tanks—147 gallons of gas and our now-customary twelve quarts of oil.

That night, we fell into another habit that was to last the duration of the trip. By the time we tied up, filled up the tanks, got the boat ready for the night, and staggered to the nearest hotel, motel, or rooming house (we eventually hit all three), it would be close to nine o'clock. Most dining rooms or restaurants in the smaller places where we stayed stopped serving at 9:00. So we would hustle into the restaurant, beg them to stay open while we had a fast shower and change of clothes, and then return in another twenty or thirty minutes.

That first night, and every subsequent night, we were so tired from the sun, wind, and the day out on the water that we simply passed out as soon as we lay down after dinner. Sleeping definitely was not a problem. Sunburn, however, was. When we started out the second day we were bright as lobsters from sun- and windburn, and we lathered up with SPF 20 sunblock.

This, however, opened up another problem, which we realized later in the day. As we sweated in the boat, the sunscreen would leak down into our eyes, and it would sting terribly as we sped along at 45 miles per hour. The problem was that, whether you were driving or—on the inside passages—navigating, you really couldn't close an eye. And if you wiped it with your hand it made it worse, since your hand obviously had the stuff on it to begin with. Subsequently, we didn't put sunblock on above eye level, which made for incredible forehead burns later on.

That day we were very stiff, much the same feeling as on the second day of a ski vacation. Everything ached. The good news was that the morning started bright and hot as we headed out into the ocean. After a few hours, the seas picked up and we started pounding uncomfortably, so we headed in at Jacksonville.

As you come into the Jacksonville harbor you are confronted with two channels leading back to the ICW. The one on the left appears the larger, so we sped up to it— only to realize that it led directly into a restricted Navy base, complete with an aircraft carrier, a destroyer, and several smaller ships. As we swept along—still at 40 miles per hour or so in our ocean-racing speedboat—all of a sudden a very serious looking Navy workboat with sailors carrying M-16s sped out, horn blaring, lights flashing, to intercept us. As one sailor started to aim his rifle in our direction, the others waved us off. We turned around immediately, as immediately as anyone has ever turned around a Tempest 38, and promptly negotiated our way up the other channel. Then we relaxed a bit.

The weather worsened as we approached Fernandina, and by the time we pulled in for gas just after noon, we were getting a few sprinkles. Unfortunately, what is a light rain on land is a disaster when you're going 45 miles per hour in an open speedboat without a windshield or any protection. The raindrops, hitting your forehead and face, sting like little blocks of ice. Unpleasant.

Because of the weather, we stayed on the Waterway through beautiful marshlands, shallow sounds, and bays as it wound its way north like a snake. We traded off driving and navigating since the many turns and the shallow water required constant vigilance and close attention to the chart.

We quickly realized we had a chart problem. Before we left I had stocked up with offshore charts and *Waterway Guide* charts for the entire trip. The *Waterway Guide* charts, however, unfold from each page in three or four large folds. This makes sense in a sailboat or a trawler, but we soon found that we couldn't unfold the pages on the speedboat without them flying all over the place like confetti. To turn a page or fold—about every ten miles—meant you had to duck down to the deck, out of the wind. At one point I accidentally managed to open the entire book, and twenty pages or so ended up streaming around my head. If we lost a page we would be in big trouble, so I threw the entire book to the deck, and, kneeling on it, tried to piece it back together, a process that took fifteen minutes. "Slow down," I yelled to Berton, who was greatly amused at the ridiculous scene. (His turn came later on.)

Worried about our gas—we still weren't sure about our consumption or our capacity—we pulled into Thunderbolt Marina, just south of Savannah, Georgia, in the late afternoon. A large marina, Thunderbolt has the reputation of being one of the best stops on the ICW. Unfortunately, this wasn't their day, because only after we tied up and tried to pump in some gas did we realize that their gas pumps didn't work. We eventually took on 147 gallons at the Fountain Marina almost next door—but all the down time spent tying up, negotiating at the pump, and leaping for the head ate up an hour or so.

At Savannah, we headed outside in the ocean, the weather clearing, and ran up to Charleston, South Carolina. This was indeed boating at its best—blue skies, warm weather, the seas flattening down as the evening wore on, the Tempest just loping along. We were almost totally by ourselves, seeing only a few commercial fishing boats along the way.

The sensation of aloneness, of just you and the boat on

the ocean, is an incredible high. You just start to smile to yourself, to become enveloped in a tremendously good feeling. Dolphins leaping off the bow every ten minutes or so completed the picture.

The ocean, however, is the ocean, and a crackling announcement from the Coast Guard on Channel 16—saying that a sailboat about fifteen miles offshore was taking on water and in trouble—was a sobering reminder of its dangers. A few minutes later the Coast Guard said it was going to the rescue.

Fighting the setting sun, we sped into Charleston's harbor at 8:20, Fort Sumter and American history on the left, the city spreading out ahead. We pulled into Ashley Marina, a wonderful spot close to downtown, just as the sun dropped—a yellowish ball, looking like an onion bisected by a few clouds. By the time we checked into the Charleston Inn next to the marina, a perfect half moon was up in a cloudless sky.

We got off to an early start the next morning, but the stiffness and the aches were getting worse. Sleeping was easy; getting up—usually not a problem—was difficult. I felt as if I were brain-dead. But we were getting used to the boat. We had written off the compass as totally useless, and the loran seemed spotty. But the Tempest and the twin Evinrudes were behaving perfectly, although, since the fuel gauge didn't work, we were worried about gas. From the previous days' experience, we figured we had a three-hour, 150-gallon range, not enough for a long trip. As we found out later, it wasn't enough, period.

It was another beautiful, sunny morning as we left Charleston, and I drove us out into the ocean, into the golden reflections on the water from the morning sun. We headed directly into the glow, cruising easily at 45 miles per hour, settling into the good-feeling envelope again. But then the wind picked up to 15 knots or so on the nose and we were bouncing around.

Crouching down, Berton checked the charts, but there was no place to come in—although the ICW was parallel to the coastline, only about half a mile away. We kept going, and the going kept getting worse. Finally, spotting what might be an opening in the beach through his high-power binoculars, Berton motioned to the coast. There was a small cut, about 10 yards wide, leading into a small bay with some boats at anchor. If we could get into the bay, we could get back to the ICW. But the water obviously was extremely shallow; waves were breaking over sandbars to the left, right, and dead ahead.

At this point, the ocean was no longer an option, so we had to pick our way in. Unfortunately, no other boats were coming in or going out. At about 7:30 on a Saturday morning, the only signs of life were half a dozen fishermen surf casting off the beach. We had two choices: First, to come in on plane, trimming up the tabs and drives to reduce our underwater surface to a minimum, or, second, to try to float in with the tide. The downside to running on plane at 30 miles per hour or so was that if we did run aground the boat would get stuck like a spear in the sand; we'd never get it off. So, picking my way gently around the sandbars, I throttled back to idle and, alternately working the gears into forward and neutral, let the boat float into the bay. We hit bottom once, but then the next wave pushed us a few feet ahead into deeper water. It took half an hour for the thirty-eight-foot speedboat to idle silently into the inlet, and by then dozens of fishermen were lining the banks.

On the ICW, we were bothered by a growing vibration;

it seemed like we had a propeller problem. We also had a bridge problem. In the early afternoon we came to a dead stop at a closed bridge—one that comes down to the water—south of the Charlotte River inlet. I blew the horn. I blew the horn several more times, a long and a short, the bridge-opening signal. Nothing happened. No signs of life on the bridge—or anywhere else, for that matter. We were in the middle of nowhere.

Finally, hoping to find some way of opening the bridge, I nosed the Tempest up to it and Berton jumped off the bow. I should have backed out, but I waited there to pick him up. Before I realized what was happening, the current swung the boat gently broadside to the bridge. This wasn't a problem, except that there were only about two feet of clearance on either side of the boat. By not paying attention, I had managed to get us wedged against a non-opening bridge with the current holding us tight. Having awakened the bridge keeper from a sound sleep, Berton returned to the boat. After ten minutes of tugging and pulling, of backing and turning (both props were right-handed, so we really couldn't spin the boat), we were free again.

Back on plane, the vibration was getting worse. Clearly the propellers needed attention. The time seemed right at Shallotte Inlet, where we could run the bow up on a shallow sand beach and wade back to work on the props. Berton, who has done this many times before, managed to change both props quickly, using the two new ones we had stored in the bow. It turned out that one of the blades on the starboard prop had almost sheared itself in half— a clean cut with no dents. We hadn't hit anything; somehow the prop had suffered some kind of metal fatigue that would have spun the entire blade off fairly soon if we hadn't stopped. Once we changed one prop, of course, we had to change both since the new ones were shaped differently from the old ones. The beached speedboat drew something of a crowd—and many kind offers of help and tools.

A tip from experience: When you start a trip, make sure you have all the appropriate tools, including many cotter pins of many sizes (we almost couldn't change the second prop for lack of a cotter pin), ball peen hammers, vise-grips, pliers and almost anything else you can think of. In fact, if you can think of it, you probably need it.

The new props cured the vibration problem and, running offshore later in the day, they also took care of much of the pounding problem. The boat definitely took on a better running attitude with the new props.

With the stop for the props and our troubles at the bridge, we were now running behind schedule, and we finally sped into Beaufort, North Carolina, just after dark, using the searchlight on our radar arch to supplement the running lights. We arrived at low tide and Berton, once he pulled himself up on the dock, was so tired he couldn't move. After I handed up our bags we just stood there for a while before trudging down the street to a motel.

The next morning the weather was beautiful again, but we were beat. As we climbed in the boat we turned to our second offshore chart, this one covering from Cape Hatteras, North Carolina, to Cape Sable, Nova Scotia, giving us a strong sense of progress. Until now our unspoken feeling was that anything could happen at any time and that would be that. Now, the trip was serious. We had already come too far; this was going to be a trip to the finish. We had come past Cape Fear and now were just inside Cape Hatteras—and we were heading for Maine.

Our driving had turned into a routine. A morning person, I usually started out, while Berton, definitely not a morning person, took over later in the day. This worked well, not only because of our personal preferences; Berton is a better driver than I am, and if we needed to make time late in the day, he could handle it faster.

As we pulled out of the Beaufort dock, we were increasingly frustrated by not knowing the boat's gas capacity. The tank was full, but we had a long way to go before we could fill up again.

Running through the Carolinas, we were continually amazed at the number of people out using their boats—people and boats of all sizes and shapes. Clearly the area was a boating and fishing paradise. We sped along up enormous bays and sounds, through huge, sprawling areas of shallow water, often aiming for markers way off on the far side of a large body of water. The weather was hot and hazy, and the white quality of the day made it hard to pick up the markers or a far shore.

As time went by, we also realized we were reaching the end of our gas. We had already been running for three hours, our mental limit, and the defective gauge, which had been hovering on half-full for almost all day, suddenly dropped like a rock to empty. We desperately checked our charts and *Waterway Guides*, but there was no place to stop. Running under 5000 rpm to conserve fuel, taking the turns gently, flat, to keep the boat level, hoping not to empty the tanks, I aimed us across one final sound and into a narrow channel. We could see a large bridge about a mile ahead; Coinjock Marina and gallons of gasoline were just on the other side.

Then it was all over; we ran out of gas. Not a sputter, not a cough, we simply died. I tried restarting a few times, but it was pointless to run down the batteries. So here we were in a beautiful, sleek, ocean-conquering speedboat, on our way from Miami to Maine, floating along on dead empty. This was really ridiculous; I felt extremely stupid.

As luck would have it, a couple were out fishing nearby in their small cruiser *Sand Dollar* from Virginia Beach. When they realized our predicament, they offered to tow us the mile or so to the marina. It took a while to arrange the lines—to keep them out of *Sand Dollar*'s prop—but eventually they pulled us in, casting us off quite professionally at the dock. As we shouted back and forth across the water, I could only hear that *Sand Dollar*'s captain's name was Bill. A Good Samaritan if there ever was one.

At Coinjock, the Tempest took exactly 185 gallons, which settled the capacity question. After refueling, and now considerably behind schedule, we headed up the ICW to Norfolk, hoping to continue on offshore from there. But the short stretch of ICW from Coinjock to Norfolk is intersected by several bridges—and even a set of locks—that open only on set hourly or half-hourly schedules. By the time we hit Norfolk it was almost 5:00, and then we had to crawl through the port off-plane because it was the annual Harborfest celebration.

Not a good day. And, of course, it got much worse after we hit that bad weather outside the bridge. After our brush with the twelve-foot seas, the 35-knot winds, and the Coast Guard's warning, we headed back for the only opening we could find on the north side of the bay—an opening that, fortunately, gave us protection while still offering an adventure of its own.

This was our introduction to the Virginia Inside Passage, the VIP. At the time we sped into it, we had little choice.

We couldn't stay outside in the ocean, and going all the way back to Norfolk (a long way) and then heading up the Chesapeake Bay didn't seem attractive. For openers, the Chesapeake goes the wrong way—too far west—and then you have to make a long circle back through the C&D Canal and down the Delaware Bay just to get to Cape May, New Jersey. Our plan had been to take the direct route: offshore, pretty much on a straight line, from Norfolk to Cape May.

The little-traveled VIP made much more sense than getting bashed around offshore. It was tricky running, in narrow channels and shallow water with the markers often few and far between, but at least we didn't have to worry anymore about getting killed. The worst thing that could happen was that we'd run aground—and walk off the boat.

As it turned out, we maneuvered the S-turns and the slalom runs and the marshes and tiny inlets to arrive at Wachapreague, Virginia, a tiny fishing hamlet, just as the sun was going down. After we tied up the boat, two men from the Coast Guard came by in a small Boston Whaler, obviously skeptical that we were who we said we were and that we had come from where we said we had come from. Not that many speedboats tie up at Wachapreague at night, with the drivers claiming innocently that they're on a little run from Miami. Finally, politely but quizzically shaking their heads, they left.

That night we slept in two rooms on the second floor of a house two blocks from the marina—and were kept up almost all night by a party of fishermen downstairs. An ill omen.

Although I have sailed to Bermuda and raced a Cigarette speedboat—with Berton—from San Francisco to Los

Angeles, the next day seemed like the longest day I have ever spent on a boat. Mindful of the conditions we had hit outside Norfolk the previous evening, I charged up our handheld radio and tucked my personal strobe light inside my shirt. I kicked myself for not bringing my float coat; Berton immediately donned his. On the boat at 6:30 AM, we broke out the raft, placing it within easy reach in the cockpit, and put the life jackets on the deck behind us. I was very sorry we didn't have an EPIRB emergency beacon. Another tip: If you think you might need safety gear, you need it. Take everything with you.

This was no longer a joyride. We were out of the south and the eighty-degree weather. It was cold. The wind was still blowing hard at 35 knots, and small craft warnings were flying all the way up the coast. This was serious. It also was something we were going to do by ourselves— no other boats were out.

If you want to lose weight, forget about Jane Fonda's workouts. Drive a speedboat offshore from lower Virginia to Connecticut some day. Breakfast at the marina was two Twinkies and a Diet Pepsi; it's all there was. Lunch was nuts from a tin on the boat and another Diet Pepsi. We now gave it our all—total concentration—as we sped up the coast. We needed to make time today to make up for all the downtime the day before. And we did.

The Tempest settled into a steady rhythm of 45 miles per hour at 5800 rpm in three-foot seas that just kept us moving closer and closer to New York. The loran, which hadn't performed well when we were in the ICW, now was right on target, and we simply fell into a groove a few miles offshore of watching the miles go by.

We saw wild horses on the beach of Chincoteague, exactly where they're supposed to be, and, as the day wore on, we even saw dolphins leaping gracefully off the Jersey coast.

After we crossed the mouth of the Delaware Bay and were opposite Cape May, my mind, almost a total blank, started reciting, *"Take me home, take me home,"* in rhythm with the sounds of the boat. We had a confused three- to five-foot heavy chop up to Atlantic City, where we pulled in just after noon for gas. By this time we had our case-of-oil, fill-the-tank act down pat, and we were in and out of the marina there in about fifteen minutes.

The seas got worse coming into New York, but that, after all, was home. At the very worst, we had made it from Miami to New York City in one piece. But, after a false stop for gas at the 23rd Street Marina (they only had diesel), we kept on, pushing up the East River and Long Island Sound to a fast refueling in Mamaroneck, New York.

The weather was threatening, the seas were up, and we were late. We had to keep going if we were going to get to Maine the next day. So we left Mamaroneck before 5:00, still in small craft warnings, and headed up the Sound.

About two hours later, I lost it. Driving the Tempest in three- to five-foot following seas, at 45 miles per hour, I totally lost control of the boat. It simply turned to the right as if pulled by some force off the bow, carving a fairly steep right turn that I had no power to stop. Trying not to panic, I simply cut the throttles as fast as I could, while the boat slowed to a stop—fortunately already past the broaching position and heading back the way we had come. Berton and I, more than a little worried, simply stared at each other. We kept going for another hour, finally pulling into Old Saybrook, Connecticut, at 7:30 PM—after thirteen hours on the boat.

The next morning, our last morning, was dark and gloomy with storms threatening all around us. For the first time, Berton beat me out of bed. At 6:30 I couldn't move. At 7:15, as we pulled out of Old Saybrook, my eyes were so red and swollen from the wind and spray that I couldn't focus on the chart. Neither could Berton, although we both managed to focus after we took the first wave of cold green water over the bow. Something about being drenched at 45 miles per hour at 7:30 in the morning—knowing that you'll be doing this all day—tends to wake you up.

Like the day before, this too was a no-food performance. This time there was no breakfast at all, since the marina was still closed when we left and there wasn't anything left on the boat. Lunch, when we stopped in the Cape Cod Canal, was a doughnut and another Diet Pepsi.

But first we were wading through yet another day of small craft warnings, of being the only boat out on the water, of worrying about the impending storm and the water cascading over the bow in three- to five-foot seas. We still didn't know if the bilge pump worked.

Little things like that, at this point, didn't matter. We were going to make it to Maine this day if we had to jump overboard and pull the boat through the water with our teeth. We set the throttles, navigated by the loran (now working perfectly), tried to keep the charts from disintegrating in all the water coming aboard, and sped off. The seas were so rough that the raft was sliding all over the cockpit.

Buzzards Bay lived up to every ounce of its lousy reputation. The sea conditions were bad, and we were tired.

North of the Cape Cod Canal the seas flattened out a bit, down to three feet, although the wind was on the nose. Finally, north of Boston, the seas calmed down as if the gods were rewarding us toward the end.

The weather, now fairly cold, turned frigid north of Boston, almost as if we had opened a refrigerator door. Maine must be near. Now the endurance contest was in its final stages; we didn't talk, we just counted the miles left.

We went inside at Gloucester, Massachusetts, up the canal, and then out again for the run to Kennebunkport, Maine, our final destination. For the last five miles, the whitecaps flattened out, and we simply flew into Kennebunkport with huge dark storm clouds building up behind us, chasing us all the way. It was hard to believe, but we had made it. Only at the end, as we made the turn into the harbor, did we start to get happy. Then we simply got ecstatic—ending with a warm glow that lasted for a couple of weeks. We actually had pulled this off.

Along the way, we'd had many adventures—some calm spots, some boring spots, some spine-chilling spots. We had enormous amounts of solitude—and heaps of self-reliance—and we had met a fairly heady challenge. All in all, a trip worth taking.

September, 1987

⚓

MAYDAY, MAYDAY, MAYDAY

When a freak storm hits New England, the Coast Guard goes to the rescue—and almost loses its own men, boats, and choppers.

BY JOANNE A. FISHMAN

So sudden was its onset, so violent its fury, they called it "The No-Name Hurricane." The freak North Atlantic storm began brewing off the Nova Scotia coast in the wake of Hurricane Grace this past autumn, then strengthened as it drifted southeasterly onto its deadly track. Roaring across the Atlantic Ocean, the fierce northeaster formed a surprise merger with the remnants of Grace moving up from Bermuda. Sustained 70-mile-per-hour easterly winds, reaching 90 at times, raged for some thirty-six hours over the long fetch, building mountainous swells up to forty feet topped by ten-foot wind-waves— and wreaking havoc all along the coast from Maine to the Carolinas.

As the 205-foot U.S. Coast Guard cutter *Tamaroa* headed out from her base in New Castle, New Hampshire, to resume patrolling the busy northeast fishing grounds, little did her eighty-one-member crew know that during the next three days the unpredicted storm would propel them into an incredible high-seas drama pitting all their courage and skill against the unleashed forces of nature. Going without sleep for more than sixty hours straight, they would have to persevere through three back-to-back rescue marathons in which the ferocious hurricane would claim one boat, one helicopter, one lifeboat, one life raft— and one life.

When the cutter's officers realized they were on a collision course with the brewing storm, they decided to change course. "We knew it would be too nasty to safely conduct boardings," says the *Tamaroa*'s forty-one-year-old commander, Lawrence G. Brudnicki, "and figured the fishermen wouldn't chance staying out." So instead of continuing offshore to Georges Bank, the cutter headed in for shelter, anchoring off Provincetown, Massachusetts, in the lee of the tip of Cape Cod.

Just before midnight, however, the First Coast Guard District received a Mayday call: The thirty-two-foot sloop *Satori* was in trouble in rising winds and seas ninety miles south of Nantucket. Directed to go to its aid, the *Tamaroa* was soon steaming toward the Cape Cod Canal, then out through Buzzards Bay for the run south. Built in 1943 as a World War II Navy salvage ship, the cutter is long on power and short on speed. But with the following seas, she fairly flew along at 17 to 18 knots.

In addition to the *Tamaroa*, the Coast Guard had dispatched a whole backup fleet to the scene: A Falcon jet that stayed with the *Satori* until the cutter arrived, helicopters that took turns hovering overhead, and the cargo ship *Kala Mona*, which was asked to divert to the spot and stand by. At one point, a helicopter crew tried to lower a life raft to the sailboat, but was unable to reach it in the rough winds and seas.

About 1 PM the next day, twelve hours after her departure, the *Tamaroa* found the bedraggled *Satori* limping along under auxiliary power, fast running out of fuel. Owner Ray Leonard of Portsmouth, New Hampshire, had been on his way from Portland, Maine, to Bermuda with two passengers, Sue Bylander and Karen Simpson, both of Portland, when his boat broached in the stormy seas, washing overboard such crucial gear as the life raft, life jackets, and extra fuel tanks. Worse yet, the fierce winds had blown out all the sails except for a scrap left clinging to damaged rigging, and the boat had begun taking on water, though its pumps were so far keeping up with the flow.

But the most immediate problem the *Tamaroa*'s crew encountered was one they hadn't anticipated. While the two women aboard the *Satori* were anxious to get off, Leonard was determined not to abandon his boat, which had been his home for ten years. He insisted he just wanted a tow or some fuel. "But the weather was predicted to get even worse," says Commander Brudnicki, who was well aware that if they didn't rescue the sailboat's crew within the next few hours it would also be dark, further increasing the risks, particularly with the fuel supply so low.

Over the radio, the commander tried to talk Leonard into getting off, explaining that there was no way the Coast Guard could safely tow the *Satori* in such heavy seas, nor was there any way to transfer fuel into the sailboat without getting salt water in its tanks. "And I pointed out that since the seas had washed the *Satori*'s life raft over the side," says Brudnicki, "there was a good chance one of its crew could get washed over as well." But Leonard was still reluctant to leave. There was only one thing left to do: Brudnicki called the commander of the First Coast Guard District, who declared the voyage "manifestly unsafe" and terminated it. That allowed the Coast Guard to *order* Leonard off the boat.

Brudnicki could now begin implementing the rescue operation, aided by Executive Officer Lieutenant Commander Melville B. Guttormsen, who also holds the distinction of being the Coast Guard's "ancient mariner," an honor bestowed on the officer with the longest service record. Springing into action, the *Tamaroa*'s crew set about launching the *Tam 1*, one of her two twenty-foot Hurricane rigid-bottom inflatable lifeboats powered by inboard diesels.

Led by Chief Bosun's Mate David T. Amidon, the threesome that manned the *Tam 1* were outfitted in drysuits, life jackets, and rigid helmets to protect them against blows from the lifting bridle and hook. The gear turned out to be a lifesaver. No sooner were the men and inflatable lowered into the churning sea than Amidon suddenly found himself "knocked out of the boat and hanging over the side," he says. One of the crewmen pulled him back in, but, he says, "I knew then we were in for a ride."

Amidon's plan was to approach the *Satori* from astern, pass survival suits to its crew, and once they were suited up, bring them on board the lifeboat. "But," he says, "the waves were steadily getting bigger as we were making our way to the sailboat." So, to avoid being thrown against the sloop, they were forced to pull up along its port stern quarter. As the *Tam 1* approached, a monstrous wave picked up the *Satori* and slammed it down onto the lifeboat's bow. With a sudden whoosh, "the whole bow section blew out," says Amidon. "Puff—it was gone—completely deflated." In addition, one of the forward eyes for securing the lifting bridle had been ripped out.

The Coast Guardsmen transferred the survival suits to the *Satori* passengers and backed away. With no bow on the lifeboat and with the seas now reaching as high as thirty feet, Amidon knew he couldn't approach the sailboat or take the passengers on board. "Without a bow," he says, "I couldn't follow the *Satori* into the seas" as the sloop made headway into the waves at a 45-degree angle. Even worse, the lifeboat was in danger of being swamped.

An air rescue was now the only hope, so *Tam 1* stood by as a Coast Guard helicopter was called into action. The *Satori* crew slipped into the water and the chopper lowered a rescue swimmer to help Leonard and the women get into the basket.

As the sailboat passengers were being lifted to safety, however, things got worse for the *Tam 1* when a mammoth wave crashed down, totally swamping it. "The boat just filled up," says Amidon. And even though built-in flotation kept it from completely sinking, "I was standing waist-deep in water," he says. "The only part of the boat above water was the steering wheel. The engine stalled, and my engineer and I just looked at each other. But amazingly, it started up again even though we were still submerged. Once we started going, it was like driving underwater, until eventually the boat started to drain."

Meanwhile, Amidon looked over at the *Tamaroa*, and he could see the cutter was having a tough time, too. "That 205-foot ship was like a cork in the water the way it was being pitched about," he says. "On our approach, there were times when we were level with the bridge—that's how high the waves were, which is scary. And the ship was rolling so much that at times I was looking at its bottom."

To return to the cutter, the *Tam 1* crew would have to head into the seas—again practically impossible without a bow—to come alongside. Even if they succeeded in hooking onto the *Tamaroa*'s cable, they were then apt to be tossed into the sea because of the broken lifting eye. "The hardest part," says Amidon, "was making the determination that we couldn't return to the ship."

Assessing the worsening conditions, Commander Brudnicki made the call: "The seas were now a steady thirty feet and the winds were recorded at more than 80 knots," he says. "I ended up deciding that someone would probably get hurt if we tried to get our lifeboat back." The *Tam 1* crew would have to be picked up by helicopter.

Having just watched the *Satori* passengers get pulled up from the sea to safety (with only one injury—a broken finger for Leonard), Amidon says he and fellow *Tam 1* crewmen Jeff Ruggiero and Herb Summers felt confident that the helicopter would be able to rescue them as well. "So I just shut down the boat and we jumped off the windward side," he says. As the helicopter lowered its basket and lifted the men to safety, the *Tam 1* blew away, out of sight. But with six lives saved so far, the Coast Guard was winning its battle with the storm.

As soon as the chopper left for Cape Cod, about 3:30 PM, the *Tamaroa* turned into the waves to head back, too. But it was heavy going. Against the hurricane-force winds and enormous seas, the cutter was making only two knots over the bottom even though its propeller shaft was turning at the rate of 11 to 12 knots in normal conditions.

Ironically, however, the *Tamaroa*'s lack of headway proved fortunate for the crew of yet another craft in trouble. About 9:30 that night, an Air National Guard HH–60 rescue helicopter with five airmen on board was on the verge of being forced to ditch into the black storm-tossed ocean sixty miles south of Long Island, fifteen miles from the cutter. The *Tamaroa*'s radio operator picked up a conversation between the helicopter and an accompanying tanker aircraft from which it had been refueling. "We heard the pilot say, 'We've got forty pounds of fuel left and I'm going to ditch,' " says Commander Brudnicki. "When we heard that, we turned around and headed for them."

The helicopter had been on its way back to the Suffolk Air National Guard Base in Westhampton, Long Island, after an unsuccessful attempt to rescue a singlehanded sailor on a thirty-foot sloop some 210 miles south of Nantucket. Contrary to initial reports, the chopper crew had found the yacht undamaged, though the sailor did want to get off. At that point the pilot had been reluctant to put a rescue team in the water because he was afraid he wouldn't be able to get them back. He figured the sailor was "better off staying on the boat—he could ride out the storm, and he did," says Brudnicki.

Though the helicopter had refueled three times from the tanker aircraft since taking off at 4:00 that afternoon, it needed a fourth refueling to make it home. But as the winds reached hurricane-force, "Visibility was down to zero with extreme turbulence," says the pilot, Major Dave Ruvola—conditions he knew could make him lose control of the chopper. "We were at the mercy of the turbulent air." The helicopter was unable to connect with the refueling plane and Ruvola was forced to use the little fuel he had left to make a controlled descent. With searchlights beaming, "We broke out of the clouds at two hundred feet," he says. "The waves were now forty to fifty feet high and the troughs fifty or sixty feet wide."

The airmen threw a life raft, an Eastern Aero T9, into the sea. Ruvola held the chopper ten feet above the highest wave tops while the four crewmen jumped out the door, then he followed them. But they found themselves bobbing helplessly in the mountainous seas. Though the raft deployed, the conditions were so wild most of the men could not get to it. "The wind and waves were tremendous," says Ruvola. "One guy got close—he got in but was flung out. That happened twice. Then the raft drifted away."

Though the spot was only fifteen miles from the *Tamaroa*, the going had become so heavy that it took the cutter a full four hours to reach it. In the meantime the Coast Guard launched both a Falcon jet plane, which quickly reached the airmen, spotting the strobe lights on their survival suits, and a helicopter. The chopper crew attempted a rescue, but the increasingly violent weather made an air approach impossible. The wind was so strong it blew the rescue basket back almost into the chopper's tail-rotor blade.

"Until the *Tamaroa* arrived on the scene, Major Ruvola later told me, he thought he and his crew were dead," recalls Brudnicki. "Then he saw us come over the horizon and believed they were saved. But when he was on top of a wave looking down on us, he wondered, 'How in the world am I ever going to get on that ship?'" Normally the Coast Guard would put rescue swimmers in the water with tag lines back to the ship and lower scramble nets over the side, but the commander was afraid of losing the swimmers in those conditions. And the seas were now too wild to launch another lifeboat.

"Trying to fight and maneuver the ship to pick up people was difficult," says Brudnicki. "You're at the mercy of the seas. Their intensity and power were hard to believe." The commander opted to go a couple of hundred yards upwind, turn the *Tamaroa* sideways, and "let the waves push us down onto the people," he says. In the dark, swirling seas, it wasn't till the cutter was within fifty feet of the swimmers that its crewmen were able to spot their strobe lights. The Coast Guardsmen then lowered cargo nets over both sides of the ship forward of the pilothouse.

"The *Tamaroa's* bridge is thirty-eight feet above the waterline," says Brudnicki, "but we were looking *up* at the tops of the waves. When we were coming through the seas, the waves were literally crashing over the bow with whitewater everywhere." Making the situation infinitely more risky was the fact that sixteen Coast Guardsmen had to be stationed on the bow ready to get the airmen out of the water. "We used the buddy system," says Brudnicki. "When the waves were breaking over the bow, each guy's job was to hang onto his buddy and make sure he was still there after the water receded. . . . Sometimes," he confesses, "it's easier to be out on the bow than to order others out there."

As the *Tamaroa* drifted toward the airmen, the cutter's crew could see only three strobe lights in the water—two shared by three people clustered together and one on a person floating alone. As the cutter reached the swimmers, they grabbed for the nets. "The four airmen hung on as our crew hauled them onto the ship," says Brudnicki. One had suffered a broken rib and wrist while jumping into the sea, while a second, who wasn't wearing an exposure suit, was near death from hypothermia. The fifth airman, thirty-two-year-old Technical Sergeant

Arden "Rick" Smith of Shirley, Long Island, was nowhere in sight.

The cutter crew continued to hunt for Smith throughout the night after an aircraft reported seeing some fresh green dye-marker—but to no avail. The next afternoon the *Tamaroa*, having served as the command center for the massive search—which eventually drew U.S. Navy, Air National Guard, and Coast Guard aircraft out of bases from Maine to Florida—was finally relieved by another cutter. Tragically, the search had to be called off the following day.

After dropping the four surviving airmen off on Long Island, the *Tamaroa* at last headed back toward Cape Cod to pick up her crewmen who'd been rescued off the *Tam 1* by helicopter.

On returning to port, the *Tamaroa* received a hero's welcome. As the cutter sat docked in Buzzard's Bay, a surprise visitor—Secretary of Transportation Samuel Skinner—arrived and shook the hand of every crewman, even tracking down those on watch throughout the ship, to thank them for the ten lives they had saved and to give them an accolade: a pin with the department seal and the inscription "Way To Go."

May, 1992

⚓

ACROSS THE ATLANTIC BY OUTBOARD

The firsthand account of a boatbuilder's record crossing from Newfoundland to Portugal on his twenty-six-foot skiff.

BY AL GROVER, AS TOLD TO POLLY WHITTELL

My love affair with boats began at the age of twelve. I used to work weekends fishing on the old wooden Verity skiffs that were used for decades on the south shore of Long Island. We'd come in the inlet at night when it was all whitewater—there weren't even jetties then—and these boats would go right through the breakers just like ducks.

I liked the way the Verities looked and the way they felt. So about ten years ago (after they stopped making them) I bought a 1926 model for a hundred bucks that had been sunk for two years. When we took it across a bridge on our trailer, all covered with barnacles, the tolltaker wanted to know if we'd finally found Noah's Ark. But that hull became the mold for the Groverbuilt boats I've been making in fiberglass, with some modifications, ever since.

Up to now I had done just about everything with my boats short of running them over Niagara Falls—and crossing an ocean—and felt they were pretty salty. (The Coast Guard even uses them in rescue work.) I've done plenty of coastal cruising where you always have a safe harbor to run to if the weather turns bad. But after reading a lot of books about long-distance voyaging by the likes of Joshua Slocum and Sir Francis Chichester, I began to wonder what it would be like out there, and if I had the stuff to hack it. . . . I had to find out. I needed to do something different and exciting to break the monotony of going to the shop every day for thirty-five years. I decided to try for a record crossing in a small motorboat.

Everyone thought I was crazy, of course. But when I built my present boat three years ago, I modified the basic Groverbuilt design with a transatlantic voyage in mind. I gave the boat a pilothouse that was about ten inches lower for less wind resistance and was enclosed in unbreakable, watertight Lexan, and I added extra foam and watertight compartments in the bilges and other cavities to make it virtually unsinkable. Then I really committed myself: I painted *Trans Atlantic* on the hull.

Once I had opened my big mouth it seemed like there was no way out. So I signed on Ted Burkhart, a Maine Maritime Academy graduate who is an expert navigator, and went for a test run from my home in Freeport, Long Island, out to Montauk Point. The only trouble was, somewhere along the way it seemed like the boat didn't want to turn around. The next thing we knew we were up at Block Island, Rhode Island, where everybody at Ballard's Inn was buying us drinks and toasting us for the trip to Europe that Ted had told them we were embarking on the next morning. Five days later we found ourselves in

Yarmouth, Nova Scotia—after repeats of the Ballard's performance in every port along the way—freezing cold in the summer shorts and T-shirts we had left for Montauk in. Though indeed a good navigator, Ted was a young, single guy who liked to party and I had felt obliged to accompany him on his escapades to make sure I still had a first mate on board the next morning.

I called home and begged my wife to drive up with some warm clothes, money, and anyone in the family who wanted to do a little coastal cruising (I have five children aged sixteen to twenty-nine). She complied—but not until she'd bought Ted a plane ticket home and sent him packing. She thought my chaperoning was above and beyond the call of duty and suggested that, if I really wanted to do this transatlantic voyage, I should have one of my sons crew to ensure I wouldn't take too many risks.

Based on our explorations, which had us dodging icebergs as far north as Goose Bay, Labrador, we decided that Newfoundland would be a good jumping-off point the next season. We planned to take four men in two boats—the second to be skippered to my twenty-nine-year-old son, Al Jr.—as added insurance. And instead of our standard inboard diesel power, we'd use twin sixty-five-horsepower Evinrude outboards and an additional 9.9-horsepower auxiliary motor. I felt that having three independent power plants would provide a good safety valve—plus a crossing by outboard would constitute a real first. We hoped to fulfill the founder of Evinrude Motors Ole Evinrude's one-time dream of retracing the path of the Vikings, his ancestors, back to Norway via Greenland and Iceland. The route also seemed appealing because of the relatively short hops involved.

Things didn't get off to a great start, however. As we

drove up through Maine in July, the trailer carrying the second boat jackknifed and flipped it into a ravine, causing so much damage we had to leave it behind. Then when we reached Nova Scotia, the car's transmission burned out from the heavy hauling. Now we had a wrecked boat, a wrecked trailer and a broken-down car. It seemed like a lot of bad omens—someone up there saying *don't go*. We also heard that the northern route is subject to very fierce gales and there are stretches where you don't see a living soul—or any services—for hundreds of miles.

So at the last minute we changed the entire plan. We would now take the original boat, with Al Jr. accompanying me on the first half of the trip and my second son, twenty-five-year-old Dante, on the last. With just one boat, the only realistic route where there would be plenty of shipping traffic in case we needed assistance was via the Azores. Since the first leg to Flores, the northernmost island in the chain, was more than 1,500 miles—almost three times as long as any stretch in our original itinerary—we would have to conserve fuel by running only one engine at a time and depending on the small auxiliary about half the way.

But we were about as well-rigged as we could be for a small boat. Our electronics included a Raytheon loran and radar, a depthfinder, two VHF radios, and a single sideband (SSB) radio, through which we could communicate with the Coast Guard at Governor's Island, New York (and home). We also had good emergency equipment—a fully provisioned four-man Tull life raft with an EPIRB emergency beacon, and Narwale survival suits.

One of the biggest dangers, of course, was the possibility of an explosion because of all the gasoline on board— 615 gallons at the start. But we had each of the eighteen aluminum fuel tanks individually grounded and vented. Most of them were aft in the bilges and cockpit, which was covered over by a plywood platform and watertight canvas tarp. With so much added weight there were only eight to ten inches of freeboard, so we were anxious to make some headway quickly. On top of the plywood we lashed two 150-gallon rubberized fuel tanks filled with air for extra buoyancy to help the boat right itself in case of a rollover. And stretched over these was a second canvas tarp. This arrangement (my wife's idea) really saved us in another way—by supporting the top canvas, absorbing some of the shock and spilling the water when the waves would crash over the stern. Otherwise we easily could have been swamped.

Our provisions included 100 gallons of water and 120 packets of space-age meals, which could be heated with a chemical pack that automatically boils when you add water to it. With all the fuel on board, we didn't dare have a stove or matches.

After launching the boat at Pictou, Nova Scotia (since that's where the car had broken down), Al and I headed for the island of St.-Pierre just off Newfoundland's south coast. As we tied up at the dock, a couple of French sailors—delivery captains—came over to look at our little boat and ask where we were going. When I said Europe, there was this dead stare. But after we learned we were all taking the same route, we decided we'd leave together the next day. We set up a communications schedule with Captain Claude (the only name I knew him by then), who was skippering a fifty-five-foot ketch, and he agreed to run with us as closely as possible, using his diesel auxiliary whenever necessary.

The local fishermen gave us a great horn-tooting sendoff, but I took a pretty big gulp as we headed out when I realized there would be no place to hide for a long time. That first day of August was a beautiful one, though with none of the usual Grand Banks fog and no depressions around. It seemed like a good time to go. By nightfall, however, all that had changed. A full gale warning was issued. Here it was, our very first night out, and we had to get hit with a real howler.

The Grand Banks area is a very bad place to be in a storm because of fog, possible icebergs, fishing-boat congestion, and the relatively shallow water, which makes for steep, nasty, breaking seas. The gale built waves of about fifteen feet and dealt winds of 50 knots that lasted a good thirty-six hours. When the wind blew over 20 knots the boat went into a seesaw act, which forced the props out of the water. So all we could do was turn the engines off and drift. At that point we really wanted to call the whole thing off and turn back, but without power it was impossible. This was also a northeast gale, and because she was so small and light, the boat couldn't go back into the heavy winds and head seas—she could only run before them. Even if she'd had enough power, she'd have been airborne trying to buck them. We found that keeping the engines down in neutral created some drag so that we didn't need a sea anchor. Under normal conditions the engines were always reliable, even when submerged—partly because they have watertight hoods, protected air intake snorkels, and special pump-out devices in case any water does get in. We also had a tiny steadying sail, but had to keep it mostly wound around the mast because the wind was so strong it could have caused the mast, which is unstayed, to tear out.

The boat soon began taking on a lot of water somewhere below, and Al, who was seasick, had to crawl down in the bilges and fix a pump that was jammed and try to find the source of the leak. It turned out to be the through-hull discharges of the other pumps, which had become submerged and had to be disconnected and plugged. Not knowing if we'd make it through the night, we rehearsed our life-raft drill. But Captain Claude was very reassuring. He was our lifeline during some of the worst times, always standing by on the radio, saying, "No problem, no problem." He would confirm our position, stand ready to help, and wait for us if we got behind. He spoke very little English and I spoke no French, but somehow we communicated beautifully.

Just as things began to return to normal, barely a day later we were hit with a second gale—a repeat performance of the same duration and intensity. By that time we'd had it with the Grand Banks, and Claude suggested heading due south to get into the Gulf Stream (where the water is deeper and the weather generally better) as soon as possible.

When we reached the Stream the skies cleared, the seas flattened, and for about a week we made some good time, logging runs of 100 to 150 miles a day. But it was during this stretch that I did a very foolish thing. I left the cabin without my safety harness to put the auxiliary motor down, and I hadn't set the bracket release exactly right. So I was pushing and pushing with all my weight when it suddenly went down—along with all 200 pounds of me, flipping me right into the water.

When I came up the boat was about 20 feet away and drifting downwind. Al looked on in horror, because with the engines locked in a dead-ahead position (though he was able to turn them off from the cabin), it would have taken quite a bit of doing to turn the boat around. He didn't want to put them in reverse, either, for fear I'd get hit by the props. Trying not to panic, I swam madly for what seemed an eternity and was finally able to climb back on board—minus my glasses. Thank goodness it wasn't at night or in the cold water of the Grand Banks.

Otherwise, things were going pretty well now and we had almost gotten to the point where we thought the rest of the trip could be a piece of cake. That was when we got the hurricane report. Hurricane Claudette, which had passed east of Bermuda, was heading east-northeast toward Flores Island at more than 25 knots. We were heading east-southeast, also toward Flores, at only 5 or 6 knots and were right in its path. There was nothing we could do. We didn't have the speed to outrun it; we couldn't turn back against the prevailing winds; and we *had* to reach Flores—still over 100 miles away—soon because we were very low on fuel.

As the atmospheric conditions began to deteriorate, we were unable to get accurate loran readings and weren't sure of our position. The SSB went out as well, because the batteries were weak from running off the auxiliary engine (which had only a small generator) to conserve fuel. The VHF, which draws less, was useless too, since we saw no ships to hail during our three to four days of the storm. In our last communication with Claude before losing him, we knew we were really in trouble when— for the first time—he admitted, "*Now* we've got a problem." We didn't have detailed charts for Flores either, because we hadn't originally planned to take the Azores route.

The closer we got to Flores, the more intense the hurricane's effects became. The worst of three days that the storm lasted was August 16, when we were at about 39 degrees north, 34 degrees west, on the hurricane's northwest edge roughly seventy-five miles from its center. As the seas built up and it really began to blow, we again had to turn off the engine and could only drift. In the daytime the sky was very dark and would periodically break into squalls and drop buckets of rain as thick black clouds flew quickly by. From the bottoms of the troughs we looked up at waves towering some twenty-five feet with five feet of foam on top that would come tumbling down, hissing and roaring, and wash over the boat. The sound of these steamrollers was pretty scary to a new guy like me out there. If we opened the little top hatch for air, we'd get soaked—we were like a submarine. The wind shrieked to almost 65 knots with gusts of 70, whipping the antennae so violently against each other they sounded as if they'd break. Worst of all were the occasional confused waves that would slam us broadside without warning. They'd hit with an incredible jolt that sounded like a gun going off, and toss us up on beam-ends. I kept saying to Al, "I just don't know how much more of this the boat can take."

We were literally bobbing and weaving like a cork or a Ping-Pong ball. But I actually think that is why we survived—because of the boat's ability to roll with the punches due to her lightness (about 8,000 pounds) and lack of resistance to the force of the wind and waves. Once the power was off, she would just run with them. With most of her windage forward in the superstructure plus a very small rudder and keel aft that held the stern straight, the bow swung forward downwind as soon as the wind got too strong. Because her stern was very narrow, with little surface for the seas to grab onto, the skiff surfed down the waves till they ran right by. A couple of times she scared us, though, when she got running faster than the seas, which could have made her pitchpole when we hit the troughs. I think the main reason we never had a rollover was because of the rounded bilge which, rather than catching, just skidded before the waves like a piece of driftwood.

You get to a point where—after wishing you had never started and doing a lot of praying and promise-making ("I'll do the following five thousand things to improve myself")—you are so exhausted you become kind of punchy or numb. You're too tired to do any more, you feel there's nothing more you *can* do, and that whatever is going to happen is going to happen. So you just conk out for a while, but always with one ear cocked for any sign of the wind letting up.

Finally the storm began to die down, but we still couldn't determine where we were in relation to Flores, and we had only 50 or so gallons of fuel left. I called and called on the VHF, and finally the captain of a Portuguese fishing vessel—Carlos Onastasio of the 200-foot *Conçeicão Viharinho*—came back in broken English. "Are you crazy or what?" he asked, but said he'd change course and come see us if we needed help. He tried to float us a chart, but the seas were still too choppy. So he gave me the true course to the island, the number of miles and the approach, then notified the port captain we were coming. What a beautiful guy.

When we arrived in Flores about ten o'clock that night there were no lights, but the port captain and several members of a fishing family named Augusto were on hand with flashlights to guide us in and help us tie up. The Augustos took us to Mass the next morning, then invited us to a big cookout of grilled sardines for about fifty people. Claude arrived the next day with damaged spreaders. And though I'm not in the habit of hugging men, I just grabbed that little guy and picked him right up off his feet when he stepped on the dock. The gas station was able to sell us enough fuel to get to the next island. Meanwhile, Al flew home and my son Dante joined me for the last leg—a 1,000-mile run to Lisbon—and we departed.

We still needed fuel, so we stopped next at Horta on the island of Faial, where we actually had to get an export license to buy our 600 gallons. Meantime we visited a famous bar called Peter's Sport Cafe, where sailors from all over the world congregate and paper the wall with pictures of their sailboats. Now there's a twenty-six-foot motorboat among them. The next stop was Ponta Delgada on San Miguel, the capital of the Azores. There must be a hundred bars there, and Claude had to make sure we didn't miss any. He'd always introduce me as an "American hero" and we'd get in free. He was a very funny guy, always kidding us about our load of fuel. Every time he heard a sonic boom he'd say, "There goes Grover." Then we started kidding Claude about his stormy "girlfriend" Claudette.

Our final leg to Lisbon was so glassy calm you could have water-skied all the way. We made almost 800 miles in only five days. As we emerged from a fog bank nearing the coast of Portugal, these beautiful 100-foot-high reddish clay cliffs came into view, and I shook Dante, who was asleep, shouting, "There's Europe, do you believe it? I never thought we'd see it."

"Looks like Block Island to me," he cracked. Heading a few miles south, we followed some big ships into the mouth of the river leading to Lisbon Harbor. We arranged by radio to be met by the Portuguese Evinrude distributor, who hosted a great reception.

Our voyage of almost 3,000 miles had taken thirty-three days, twenty-six of them at sea. Beyond the satisfaction of completing the crossing, and being told by the *Guinness Book of World Records* people that we were probably indeed the first outboard boat to make a basically unassisted transatlantic crossing, the voyage also brought me much closer to my sons. I found that being in a situation where we were totally dependent on one another gave me more confidence in them than ever before.

Upon returning home (by air) a week later, we received a congratulatory letter from President Reagan, and the mayor of Freeport declared "Grover Day," with a big welcome-back parade. In addition to all the strangers who came out of the woodwork along the way to help us whenever we were in trouble, I think we had a lot of spiritual support from our townspeople throughout the voyage. Next to our shop we have a little chapel where our family hosts Sunday services, and many people have said they were praying for us out there. Above the altar, which is fashioned out of a little boat with cross-trees for a cross, is a passage from Psalm 107 that reads: "Some went down to the sea in ships . . . [in] a stormy wind [and] sea . . . they reeled and staggered like drunken men and were at their wits' end; then they cried to the Lord in their trouble . . . and He caused the storm to be still . . . and guided them to their desired haven. Let them give thanks." That pretty well sums up how it was. And boy, did we give thanks.

December, 1985

⚓

BLOOD, SWEAT & TEARS

MB&S's women's team tackles the 'Round London Boat Marathon—the event that makes you carry your boat almost as much as it carries you.

BY LOUISA RUDEEN

"You must be mad."

When *Motor Boating & Sailing* Art Director Erin Kenney and I arrived in England to take part in the Carlsberg 'Round London Boat Marathon, that's the reaction we got from the British, particularly the women we met. Crazy or not, we were determined to be the first all-women American team to enter the competition.

The 'Round London Boat Marathon is a highly unusual rally run by Len Britnell, commodore of the London Motorboat Racing Club, and his wife Edie. The event got its start, as the Britnells tell it, when two *Daily Express* newsmen were on an extensive pub crawl in north London. Many of the pubs looked out on canals, which gave the reporters an idea. "They rang us up and said, 'We think we can get all the way 'round London by water," Len Britnell says.

The Marathon soon took shape as a grueling endurance rally in which two-person crews in small inflatable dinghies with 3- to 5-horsepower outboard motors must circumnavigate one of the world's largest cities via the Thames River and interconnecting canals, in two days. Furthermore, the contenders are not allowed to use the still-operating canal lock system, but instead must get out and portage their 100-plus-pound boats and motors around the twenty-four locks they encounter along the way.

Erin and I were entered in the sixteenth running of the 'Round London. The first day, a Saturday, dawned in typical London fashion—rain sluiced down from the heavens into the dark ribbon of the Thames. Despite the grayness of the morning, the scene at Putney, on the bank of the river, was colorful. A hundred teams of Marathoners, sporting everything from punk ripped jeans to full fatigues and purple berets (the entrants from the 10th Para), swirled around their brightly hued inflatables. Our uniform: red Musto drysuit bottoms and Offshore jackets; very toasty. We also had to wear helmets—when we asked why, one wag said that when we passed through Brixton, delinquent youths might drop rocks on us from the bridges.

A band struck up a lively tune from the mobile sound stage. "They've been told not to play 'Singing in the Rain,' " said Derek Lloyd, our British team manager.

A powerboat racer and navigator, Derek had a few last words of advice for us. "Stay close to the right-hand bank of the Thames. The current should be a little less powerful there than in the middle." The tide had just turned, which meant we would be battling an incoming 6-knot current.

We trusted that our 4-horse-power Mercury outboard would be equal to the task.

"We've had it this wet before, but not much," Britnell said at the drivers' meeting. As he explained about "hidden checkpoints" where our times would be noted in rally fashion, I studied our competitors. There were only three other women's teams. Quite a few mixed teams were in evidence, but the male halves of those partnerships were all big bruisers. *We must be mad*, I thought.

Still, I was more resolved than ever to see the Marathon through. When our starting signal came, Erin and I ran to our boat, pulses pounding. We slid it into the river, climbed in, started the motor, and headed up the Thames.

"They weren't kidding about this current," Erin said, giving the outboard more throttle. I leaned on the bow of the Avon Rover 2.80, keeping the inflatable as flat as possible, which seemed to make it go faster. I also kept a sharp eye out for propeller-busting debris in the water.

The Thames was impressive, with its wide girth and high embankments on either side. But it wasn't until we reached Lambeth Bridge that the full import of what we were doing sank in. As we spewed out from under its arches, there were the Houses of Parliament and Big Ben on the opposite bank. The Marathon was going to show us London from a unique perspective. We were rallying through history.

The dome of St. Paul's Cathedral lay around a bend in the Thames, and beyond it, the Tower of London. Cut into its massive seawall was the Traitor's Gate, where royal prisoners were once brought by barge. We passed beneath Tower Bridge, its dark bulk relieved by red double-decker buses speeding merrily across it. Then we

started looking for Limehouse, the entrance to the north-
bound Regent's Canal.

Derek met us there, waving madly. The only problem
was that he was fifteen feet up, and that was where we
and our boat had to go. We attached lines to our inflatable
and motor, and as other teams attempting the same feat
bounced into us, we clambered up the slippery ladder set
in the wall, and hoisted everything to the top. Then we
lay back on the grass, panting. We were worn out already,
and the locks still lay ahead.

Motoring through the calm waters of the canal was
lovely. Spring had come early to London, and blossoms
bordered the towpath. The rain lifted, prompting couples
to come out for a stroll. Our fellow Marathoners motored
next to us, chatting. Bigger vessels cruised by—brightly
painted craft that served as homes for the "water gypsies"
of the city.

But each time we came to a lock, things turned ugly.
Erin and I would have to jump out of the boat, haul it
onto the bank, pick it up by the handles Avon had in-
stalled on the bow and stern, and carry it around the lock.
We switched positions often because the one carrying the
motor would invariably batter her hip against it. Teams
would pass us on the portage—muscular fellows who
could balance an outboard on one shoulder. It was misery,
but we kept going.

Eight locks along, we came to the entrance of Islington
Tunnel. I switched on our flashlight, and we ventured
into its inky depths. I thought of the old boatmen who
used to "leg" the barges through this very tunnel. They
would lie on boards hooked onto the sides of the boat
and walk along the tunnel wall in their hobnailed boots.

On one portage, we lugged the inflatable through Camden Town, where shoppers in the outdoor market stopped to stare, but a band of street musicians kept right on playing—even when we dropped the boat on the guitar case that lay open to receive tips.

Maida Vale Tunnel swallowed us up, and when we emerged, Marathon officials called to us to cut our engine. We could see Little Venice, the aptly named area that was to be our overnight stop, but we had to paddle a thousand yards to get to it. Our muscles protested with each stroke, but slowly we inched our way home.

Sunday morning we woke up in our hotel black and blue, but in fine spirits. We had gotten this far, and we were determined to go all the way. After the restart, we paced ourselves with Jim and Lynne Garner, a father and daughter who were very serious about the Marathon. "We've been in the 'Round London ten times," Jim said. He and Lynn were clocking themselves to make sure they didn't exceed the rally speed limit of 4 knots on the canals. Other contestants interpreted the speed restriction more loosely. Mark Faul and Robert Sangster in boat number 100 roared up through the pack until they had passed the front-runners, then popped into a waterside pub for a pint of ale.

After several shorter portages, we reached the fearsome "Hanwell Flight" of locks. Derek met us at the top lock, and warned us that this was going to be, as he put it, "a bit of a drama." We would have to carry the inflatable past all six locks, rather than motoring between them.

We took the engine off and put it in the boat for better balance. I took the stern and Erin the bow. Our backs and arms still ached from the day before. Tears of frustration came to our eyes.

But yard by painful yard, we pressed forward. Finally,

we looked up and saw only sparkling water, not a lock in sight. With triumphant whoops we shoved the boat into the canal, charging off at full throttle to try to make up some of the time we'd lost.

Brentford Lock, which led back into the Thames, was our last hurdle. There was a long drop in water level between the lock and the river. Exhausted Marathoners were simply heaving boats off the wall, some jumping in after them. Their turtled inflatables and water-soaked engines convinced us that was not the best way to go. Using a line, we lowered the boat first, then the motor down to it, and we were off and away along the Thames.

The nightmare was behind us now. The sun was out, birds sang, and sailboats with big-bellied spinnakers raced around us. Erin and I toasted each other, saying, "Here's to you—for being tough."

Back at Putney, we jumped out of the boat to hug Derek and his wife Jane, who sprayed us with Champagne. Len Britnell gave us the news that not only had we made it all the way 'round London, we had also come in fifty-eighth out of one hundred entries. It was a good showing, considering that many of our competitors were veterans of multiple Marathons.

"Right after they finish, they all swear they'll never enter again," Britnell told us. "Then a few months later, they call and say they'll be back next year. He predicted that we, too, would return. Erin and I just looked at each other.

Would we enter another 'Round London? If we do, we must be mad.

June, 1988

⚓

OVERBOARD

A blue marlin, caught during a high-stakes tournament, suddenly pulls an experienced fisherman off the boat to his death.

By PETER WRIGHT

The strike, when it came, was fast and without warning—a "crash strike," as big-game anglers describe that kind of sudden, almost explosive, attack on a bait, with none of the stalking cat-and-mouse behavior that blue marlin sometimes display. Angler Gray Ingram grabbed the rod and got into the fighting chair.

While Ingram fought the fish, mates Chris Bowie and Ronnie Fields got everything ready. In the cockpit, the washdown hose was coiled and hung up. There were no gaff ropes, stray leaders, baits, or anything else on the deck to disturb Bowie's footing when he took the leader in his gloved hands to bring the fish alongside the boat after Ingram had wound the line up to the connecting swivel to which the leader was attached.

"We knew it was a blue," says Alan Fields, the captain, "but we couldn't tell exactly how big. It fought like a good-sized tuna, dogging it and not jumping, but I knew it was a blue because I saw the strike."

It was 9:30 AM on the fourth day of the thirty-sixth Annual Big Rock Blue Marlin Tournament out of More-head City, North Carolina. Gray Ingram's gleaming fifty-two-foot custom sportfisherman *Trophy Box*, one of almost 200 boats in the competition, was sixty miles offshore in the Gulf Stream. The weather was perfect, with bright blue skies and calm seas, and everyone on board had high hopes and expectations. They were all family—related by blood or marriage—or almost family, having fished together several times over the years.

Ingram had assembled one of the best teams on the Atlantic coast. At the helm was Alan Fields, fifty, a captain with over thirty years of experience. In the cockpit were Chris Bowie, twenty-nine—an experienced and respected captain in his own right—as first mate and wireman, and Fields's son Ronnie, nineteen, who was about to leave for the Azores to be the wireman on a boat seeking a world-record blue marlin. Among the handful of others aboard was Ingram's wife Kelly, who was recording the fishing action with a video camera.

Alan Fields and Bowie had fished together several times in the past, with Fields sometimes mating for Bowie in tournaments—just as Bowie was now doing for Fields, who had needed one more professional hand for the pres-tigious, high-rolling (over $500,000 in prize money) Big Rock Tournament. Bowie was as welcome for his reputa-tion as a man you could count on, and for his infectious smile, as for his experience.

He had spent the past ten years working as a mate or captain aboard charter fishing boats out of his Ocean City, Maryland, home port in the summers, and West Palm

Beach, Florida, in the winters, and had fished waters as far afield as the western Caribbean and the Pacific off Central America. He had caught over 1,000 billfish and had been the winning captain at the '87 Big Rock Tournament aboard *Midnight Hour* with a 587-pound blue marlin. He'd had his own rod and reel since the age of four. And at 5'9" and 200 pounds, he had kept the powerful, athletic build of his days as a high school wrestler.

Up to this point in the tournament, the *Trophy Box* team had caught only one white marlin and had released it. Now that a blue marlin had been hooked everyone hoped it was a keeper (over 300 pounds).

When the swivel reached the rod tip, Bowie calmly and carefully took hold of the .035-inch-diameter steel piano wire leader. When fishing for billfish, after all the line has been wound onto the reel, the "wireman," with gloved hands, grabs the wire leader, which can be up to thirty feet long, depending on the size of the line. In this case it was twenty-five feet of 300-pound-test wire, as the line was 120-pound test. Braced against the gunwale, the wireman then attempts to pull the fish to the boat to be either gaffed or released.

Anyone who has ever had to climb a rope by hauling himself up hand-over-hand can imagine how difficult it would be to get enough of a grip to pull his weight up if, instead of a rope, he had to climb a thin fishing leader. To pull or lift a heavy weight by a thin wire without it slipping through the hands requires wrapping the wire around the hands—as only a very experienced sportfishing wireman, such as Bowie, would have the expertise to do. Done properly, wrapping the leader wire will allow the wireman to apply his strength to lifting rather than trying to grasp the leader tightly enough to stop it from slipping.

A wire leader can be released by simply opening the hand with the fingers together and pointing toward the fish, whereupon the wire slides off or slips through the hand. But it is a technique that takes a great deal of practice.

As Bowie pulled the fish closer to the surface, Alan Fields, on the bridge, called out, "About 175 pounds, foul-hooked right in the middle of the back."

Fishermen using live baitfish will hook them through the dorsal spine so they can swim freely and can resist the pull of the fishing line without tiring for as long as possible. A small blue marlin such as this one, when hooked through the back rather than in the mouth, has greater pulling power, cannot be easily led, and can in fact fight like a much larger fish.

Still, even with the fish foul-hooked in the back, Bowie was able to pull it toward the boat. Since the fish was under the 300-pound-minimum acceptable weight to be boated, the crew prepared to release it. Under the rules of the Big Rock Tournament, the fish that Bowie was wiring already counted as officially released once Ingram had wound the swivel to the rod tip. But, like many conservation-minded sportfishermen today, the *Trophy Box* crew believed in tagging a fish. A small barbed tag is attached to the fish's back using a six-foot-long pole. This tag assists scientists in better understanding migratory patterns, or in age and growth studies, if the fish is recaptured. Many top pros don't feel that they have really caught a fish unless the tag is securely in place before it is released.

As the fish pulled against Bowie's muscular, straining

arms, its pectoral fins were the iridescent neon blue that signals an angry or excited state—a color never seen on a tired or beaten marlin. The mackerel bait could be plainly seen on the fish's back, right behind the highest part of the dorsal fin.

Just before the fish came into range of the tagging pole, it turned quickly and darted away from the transom of *Trophy Box*. Bowie let go of the wire, probably for fear of pulling the hook out before the fish was tagged.

As Kelly Ingram's home video shows, Bowie had been careful with his wraps, even hesitating between pulls to push the portion of the wire that he had already taken in behind him, and he let go of the wire cleanly and without a problem. It also shows that the deck was clear, with no clutter, blood or fish slime to make the footing unsure or slippery.

Now Ingram was again fighting the fish on the rod, but the marlin ran only a few feet before being turned by the reel's drag, and Bowie got the wire back almost immediately. Again he pulled the fish toward the surface. His actions as he took his wraps and cleared the wire behind himself were, once again, calm and deliberate.

Ronnie Fields stepped in behind Bowie and stuck the tag into the fish's shoulder. The marlin darted ahead, then repeated its turning maneuver of moments earlier. This time, however, Bowie did not let go of the wire. He held on as the fish streaked away from the back of the boat.

Bowie probably believed that he could easily hold a fish of that size and that it was not really necessary to let go. Since the tag was now in, it would not matter if the hook were pulled out. In fact, it would be good strategy to get rid of the fish as quickly as possible and get the baits back out without wasting any more time.

If Bowie had deliberately let go of the wire again, it might well have taken several minutes of valuable fishing time to reel the fish back in, especially since the fish still had such a lively appearance. It was time that could be better spent trolling for a bigger, perhaps prize-winning, fish.

As Ronnie Fields turned away momentarily to get rid of the tag pole before cutting the wire to release the fish, Bowie held on with his knees braced below the covering board, taking the strain with his back and shoulders. Suddenly, he was in the water.

The others on board mainly remember seeing Bowie's shoes as he went overboard. The video recorded a squeak like the one a basketball player's shoes make on a hardwood floor. With his footing lost, he first fell onto the transom covering board, then was jerked overboard into the water. His sun visor must have been pushed down over his eyes by his head-first entry. The crew saw him at the surface knocking the visor off his head as he started to turn toward the boat, then was pulled back down. He was swimming, not panicked or struggling, just below the surface with his hands outstretched together. They still expected that he would be okay.

When Bowie did not immediately come back up to the surface, Alan Fields backed *Trophy Box* toward him and called to Ingram to "pull him back up." Ingram got a couple of pumps with the rod and was pulling man and fish back toward the surface. Fields stopped backing up to avoid backing over Bowie. Then the leader wire broke at a kink six feet below the swivel.

Wearing shoes, shorts, and a T-shirt, Ronnie Fields, a strong swimmer and diver, leaped in to help his friend. He made one dive and came back up for air. He was not able to get down to Bowie, who was now thirty feet under and was being pulled deeper by the marlin. "I can't get to him," Fields shouted. But he tried again, nonetheless. In a few more seconds, Fields could see neither Bowie nor the marlin in the clear Gulf Stream water.

No one will ever know why Bowie was unable to get free of the leader wire after it broke—it was simply a freak accident, a case of tragic bad luck. If anything, it's usually difficult for a wireman to prevent the wire from slipping free through his hands after it's been cut—as anyone can attest who has ever tried to hold a wire so a photo of a fish being released can be taken.

The grieving survivors of the tragedy have had to rerun over and over the images of their friend's last few living moments. Even a careful analysis of the video that began as a fun-filled home movie doesn't answer their questions: What happened? What went wrong?

There are no obvious errors to point out. And the *Trophy Box* crew has nothing but praise for the U.S. Coast Guard's quick response to their distress call. A helicopter was immediately dispatched to the scene from a nearby naval vessel and a thorough search of the area was undertaken. Bowie's body was never recovered.

September, 1994

⚓

TANIA'S TRIUMPH

Tania Aebi, a gutsy girl from New York, sails around the world alone—to find herself.

BY POLLY WHITTELL

"Why are all these people so interested in me?" asked plucky, wide-eyed, twenty-one-year-old Tania Aebi when she completed her two-and-a-half-year single-handed sailing odyssey around the world. Aboard her twenty-six-foot sloop *Varuna*, she had been all alone at sea. But on her return to New York, she was suddenly the center of attention—an instant celebrity.

Tania appeared on all the TV and radio news programs; on numerous talk shows, including *Today* and *Late Night with David Letterman;* on the front pages of *The New York Times, The Washington Post* and hundreds of other papers, and in more than a dozen national magazines. She received a congratulatory telegram from President Ronald Reagan, who wrote: "You have tested the limits of the human spirit and set a new standard." Similar kudos came from the likes of Sally Ride, the first woman in space; from Robin Knox-Johnston, the first man to sail solo around the world nonstop; and from Robin Lee Graham, the youngest male solo circumnavigator. On the street, people would come up to shake her hand or ask for her autograph.

Clearly, Tania had captured the hearts and imaginations of sailors and nonsailors alike. For one thing, she had set a record. Although a technicality—an eighty-mile ride she gave a stranded hitchhiker as a favor from one South Pacific island to another on a side trip—may have kept her singlehanded voyage out of the official record books, she was still both the youngest person and the first American woman ever to complete a solo circumnavigation.

But the public interest went beyond any record. Tania emerged as a modern-day heroine at a time when many teenagers were making headlines only because of drug use or other criminal or scandalous behavior. Moreover, people were simply astonished that such a petite young girl as Tania—just eighteen when she set out—with so little sailing experience, in so small a boat, could succeed in a venture of such magnitude. At the start of the voyage, in fact, many people—including *Today* host Jane Pauley, who now apologized "for underestimating Tania Aebi"— had publicly expressed doubts that she would make it.

Undaunted, however, and with a rousing sendoff from friends and family, Tania set out from New York in the late spring on the first leg of her voyage. She expected to make Bermuda in ten days. It took fourteen. "Just about everything that could have happened to me happened, all on my first time out," she said. No sooner had *Varuna* cleared Ambrose Light Tower just outside New York Harbor than its engine conked out. But that didn't bother Tania. She could have turned back, of course, but that would have been too easy. So she raised the sails and pressed on, with only the wind, sun, and stars to propel and guide her.

After trying in vain to fix the engine, she was hit by a gale the second day. For two days, clouds made it impossible to determine her position by celestial navigation, while 45-knot winds and higher gusts repeatedly rammed the bow of the boat (now under trysail and storm jib) into big breaking waves that spilled water into the cockpit and flooded the cabin. Tania pumped frantically until the manual bilge pump became clogged, forcing her to resort to an electric pump that had little juice to run on because of the engine's failure.

After a brief lull, a second storm, almost as severe, kicked up. And when the skies finally cleared enough for her to get a fix, Tania learned she'd been blown almost 100 miles off course to the northeast. As if that weren't enough, she suddenly found herself becalmed, and wondered how long it would take to get *Varuna* back on track.

The next week brought better weather, and Tania was finally able to pick up Bermuda on her Radio Direction Finder (RDF) from about 200 miles away. But her problems weren't quite over. As she drew near the island, she found it obscured by haze, and when she finally located the narrow cut leading into St. George's Harbour, strong headwinds made it impossible for her to sail in. Reluctantly, she asked a fishing boat for a tow. "That was humiliating," she said, nonetheless relieved to have made port.

She hadn't felt frightened, she said, because "I knew I would make it eventually. I was mainly just ticked off that all this was happening to me already. I couldn't be scared, or I wouldn't have been able to keep my wits about me and do what I did." Getting to Bermuda in fact gave Tania more confidence—both in *Varuna* and in her own ability. "Then I knew I could really do it," she said.

Why would so young a girl want to undertake such a venture? Born and raised in the greater New York area, the oldest of four children, Tania was a somewhat rebellious teenager, thanks in part, perhaps, to having come from a broken home. By the time she graduated from New York's City As School in 1984, she had already taken college-level courses in English and history and wanted to be a writer. But she was restless and bored. "I hated school and I didn't want to go to college," she explained, "with all those long hours studying into the weekends and not getting paid for it."

Tania felt the voyage would serve as a shortcut to a writing career by providing an unusual experience to write about—from a unique point of view—and the time to do it. So she made a deal with her father Ernst, a Swiss-born SoHo artist: In lieu of a college education, he agreed to give her a boat for the trip if she'd take along her typewriter and write articles along the way.

"It was an opportunity I just couldn't afford to pass up," Tania said. "I felt that otherwise, without college, I didn't really have a future. I didn't want to spend the rest of my life as a bicycle messenger"—a job she spent several months at the previous spring in Manhattan. But she did feel the messenger job gave her some valuable experience for the voyage. "It taught me how to react quickly in tight spots," she said.

"I figured Tania would get a lot more out of this than school," said her father. Ernst Aebi himself had hitchhiked around the world at the age of twenty, earning money along the way by selling paintings and by "doing lots of odd jobs—*really* odd jobs sometimes. I was a belly dancer in a gay bar in Beirut, and I was 'The Terror of the Alps' in Japanese pro wrestling.''

Of his four children, Aebi said Tania was the only one with the right combination of character traits for the venture. "With any of the others, letting them go would be like premeditated murder," he said. He cited Tania's common sense, resourcefulness, and, in particular, her strong will and self-assurance. "She feels there is nothing she can't do," he said.

Tania's mother Sabine, for her part, was supportive as well. "I'm not a bit worried, only proud of my daughter," she said. "I have a lot of faith in her. She is very brave. When I warned her that the sea can be very cruel, she just said 'Mommy, the earth is even more cruel than the ocean.'' I told her, "That was the best thing you could have said. Go ahead—do it.' "

Tania had first begun sailing only a year before her solo voyage, when she and Ernst, also a novice, cruised the Atlantic in his thirty-eight-foot Rival sloop. "My father and I learned to sail together—by the trial-and-error method," she said. They managed to bring the boat through one particularly harrowing storm—the one that sank the tall ship *Marques* off Bermuda. As additional preparation for her circumnavigation, she took four-month courses in coastal and celestial navigation, and sailed her boat from Toronto to New York.

Varuna (named for the Hindu god of water) was designed by David Sadler, built by J. J. Taylor Yachts in Toronto, and specially modified for Tania's voyage. Based on a Swedish North Sea Folkboat design, it had an overall length of 25'6", a beam of 7'6", and a relatively light displacement of 5,400 pounds. For good tracking and stability in rough weather, it was built with a deep, full keel. "That was our main criterion," said Ernst, who supervised the project. In addition, the boat had glassed-in polyurethane foam for extra flotation. It carried 304 square feet of sail area, and, for use in ports and emergencies, had an eight-horsepower Bukh diesel engine (which actually wasn't working for much of the voyage). Its hull speed was about 6 knots. Fully equipped, the boat cost around $40,000—less than half what four years' tuition at a private college would have come to at the time.

Varuna was equipped with a Monitor wind-vane self-steering system and an Autohelm autopilot, but very few electronics. Tania departed with a depthsounder, VHF radio, short-wave radio receiver, and the RDF, adding an Argos satellite transponder tracking device only on her last leg. She had a radar reflector, but no radar. Her rudimentary navigation aids included a compass, a pair of binoculars with built-in compass, a Rolex Submariner watch, a calculator, a barometer, and two sextants, as well as a set of charts and tide tables.

"I left knowing nothing. I learned everything on this trip," Tania said. "I didn't know how to navigate until I reached the Galapagos and figured it out." Up to that point, besides getting fixes from passing ships and using the RDF for landings, "It was just pure dumb luck," she said. Using an "uncomplicated" textbook from a mail-order celestial navigation course her father had taken, she came to understand the theories during the voyage, she said, mainly "because I watched the sun and stars going up and down and saw how it all works."

Besides the usual complement of safety equipment, including an EPIRB emergency beacon, Tania also carried a fake hand grenade to frighten off intruders. And in case anyone got funny ideas about a girl alone, she had a solution for that, too: a stick-on beard.

The boat was well-provisioned with water, food (but no meat—Tania was a vegetarian at sea), cigarettes (which she planned to give up) and Transderm-V patches, which she hoped she wouldn't have to use even though she was prone to seasickness, because she found they made her hallucinate. Apart from writing, Tania had plenty of other things to keep her busy on quiet stretches—from tape cassettes and musical instruments (a guitar, recorder, and harmonica) to books and Trivial Pursuit games.

After the tough first leg to Bermuda, Tania enjoyed a relatively smooth sail to Panama, via St. Thomas in the Caribbean, where she picked up Dinghy, her cat. After a pleasant time in Panama—except for having to get six stitches in her head when she fell and cut it on the boat's side rail—Tania headed through the Canal for the Galapagos and Marquesas Islands in the South Pacific. Although "I liked every place I went," she said, those were her two favorite spots on the globe in terms of natural beauty— the Galapagos for its "volcanic, lunar landscape and wildlife, like a big zoo without cages"; and the Marquesas for their "lush, green mountains forming incredible panoramas." She also found the best sailing conditions of her voyage in this part of the world—nice Force 3 winds.

The next highlight was Tahiti, where Tania spent five months working on her boat, making new friends, and enjoying the island's tropical scenery and ambience. Sadly, her stay there was interrupted by the loss of her mother, Sabine, who died of cancer, necessitating a trip home for a week.

Soon after sailing out of Tahiti, Tania also suffered a series of mishaps—a fall that injured her hand, a bad earache, and a collision with a sixty-five-foot schooner that crushed *Varuna*'s bow pulpit. With all that had happened, she was feeling depressed by the time she arrived at her next South Pacific stop, Vanuatu. But not for long. A friend she'd made introduced her to Olivier Berner, a thirty-four-year-old Swiss geologist and cruising sailor who changed her life. "All of a sudden Vanuatu looked like the most beautiful place I'd ever seen," she said. Their romance blossomed as Tania, on *Varuna*, and Olivier, on his thirty-one-foot sloop *Akka*, began sailing the same route, though seldom in sight of each other, meeting up in ports along the way.

After exploring Australia's Great Barrier Reef, the two headed across the Indian Ocean, via Bali and Sri Lanka, where Tania's father joined them for an elephant safari. Just after they left Sri Lanka, the weather suddenly worsened and dealt Tania her first knockdown. "It really freaked me out," she said. She was hurled against the cabin ceiling when *Varuna* suddenly lurched, rolled over, and was engulfed by a wall of water. It took two days to get everything back together.

Tania's next big hurdle was the Red Sea, an exhausting endurance test against stiff headwinds that all but reduced *Varuna*'s mainsail to rags. Before she entered the Suez Canal, her father had a new sail delivered.

But soon afterward, heading into the Mediterranean, *Varuna* was almost dismasted in a collision with a giant cargo ship. As Tania emerged from a momentary trip below, she saw the ship's huge bow bearing down on *Varuna* in the dark. No sooner had its bow passed, missing the sailboat by a mere ten feet, than its stern caught *Varuna*'s forestay, slicing it in two. Though Tania was able to jury-rig the stay and limp into Crete for repairs, she found it took a long time to get over the fright.

Tania's toughest emotional moment during this leg of the voyage, however, was parting ways with Olivier in Malta, his final destination. She felt shattered, she said, as she tore herself away from "the best thing that ever happened to me."

The Mediterranean passage also proved the most difficult of all. As Tania approached Gibraltar, exhausted from maneuvering in heavy shipping traffic and from making constant sail changes, she noticed conditions getting progressively worse. "Soon the wind was howling and there was this huge lightning storm like strobe lights going all around me," she said. But since no storms were predicted, she figured it was just a passing squall, took down the sails, went below to wait it out, and inadvertently dozed off.

Then all hell broke loose, as *Varuna* was hit by a raging tempest. Suddenly, said Tania, a big wave "just picked us up, threw us down and crashed over us, filling the boat with water. It was a disaster. The water below was knee-deep and the whole inside of the boat was on top of me. I was thoroughly frightened. . . . I panicked."

Thinking this was it, she grabbed the EPIRB to put out a distress signal. But after a few seconds, "I realized I was alive," she said. So she collected herself and, finding the bilge pump clogged, began bailing out the water.

Since the wave had damaged the boat, washed away gear and knocked out the electronics, Tania was forced to put into Almeria, Spain. On the verge of throwing in the towel, she made a frantic phone call to her father, who agreed to meet her in Gibraltar with new equipment and to help repair the boat.

Once *Varuna* was ready, Tania set out from Gibraltar on the longest leg of the voyage—3,100 miles across the Atlantic—in the midst of the full hurricane season. Though she managed to miss the hurricanes during the fifty-day crossing, she was hit with two bad storms, the worst in mid-ocean. "There was a lot of wind," she said, "maybe 45 knots, and really huge seas, about twenty feet high, with big surf." During the height of the storm, *Varuna* took a series of knockdowns, which thrust the rail and bow pulpit underwater about every ten minutes. "We just kept going over and over, and the waves kept crashing down on us, totally filling the cockpit," Tania said. "For three days I was worried; for one day I was just plain scared."

Sometime after the storm, in seas that were still rough, a worried Ernst Aebi chartered a boat and set out to find his daughter—but could not. *Varuna*'s Argos transponder had gone out for a day, prompting the *New York Post* headline "Lost At Sea."

Though she was soon back in touch, Tania didn't exactly have smooth sailing for her homecoming, either. After running for four days without sleep in the shipping lanes, she had to buck bitter-cold, 30-knot headwinds and eight-foot seas on her approach to New York. In fact, in order to arrive in time for the heroine's welcome awaiting her, she had to be towed to Manhattan's South Street Seaport from the Sandy Hook, New Jersey, Coast Guard station by a forty-one-foot cutter. Her engine, again, was broken.

As Tania reached the dock, her father took the bowline and Olivier, who had flown to New York to surprise her, doused her with Champagne. "I'm happy to be home," she announced to a crowd of several hundred fans and members of the press. "It means I'm alive."

Reflecting on her voyage, Tania says what she missed the most—besides people—was Chinese food, since she had to rely mainly on foods that keep well. But sleeping was more problematic than eating. Without radar (just the reflector), Tania could get a good night's rest only in mid-ocean where there were no shipping lanes. In areas like the Mediterranean, she had rarely slept more than a couple of hours at a stretch. "The physical aspects of sailing aren't the hard part," Tania says. "The mental part is the hard part."

Besides fatigue, Tania found the most difficult problems she'd had to overcome were fear and loneliness. "I don't know if I'm that courageous," she says, "because I get scared pretty often." But, she says, "I've never been afraid of the ocean itself. I *respect* it, and I've been scared by a *storm*." Rather, she always saw the ocean "as a friend." She says she also has faith in a higher being who watches over things. "I prayed all the time," she says—"when there was lightning, for survival in a storm, for nice weather, for everything."

Tania's faith in herself grew, too, as she progressed on her voyage. At the outset, she says, she had some doubts. She saw the trip mainly as an adventure, figuring, "Well, let's just see what happens—I can always come home." She says her father's support helped boost her confidence. "He kept telling me I could do it."

Olivier agrees that Tania has what it takes: "She is really strong," he says, and overcomes fear, "because she believes things will go right."

"Now I know I can do whatever I set out to do," Tania says. Basically, she says, "I learned how to fend for myself.

You learn from the problems. Maybe my hard moments were harder than other people's. But that makes life richer, and makes the good moments so much better.''

There were times, Tania admits, when she felt so discouraged, or even bored, that she wished the trip were over. ''But if I had quit somewhere along the line, I knew I would think all the rest of my life, 'Why did I stop?' I *had* to finish.''

Loneliness—and homesickness—also plagued the solo sailor off and on. But Tania is a free spirit. ''I like the feeling of being totally independent,'' she says, adding that she never felt lonely while she was out on the ocean, ''because you're in absolute solitude and there's nobody there, no temptations. It's only on land, watching people talking to each other, having a good time when you have no one,'' that she would feel lonely, left out. Still, she always wound up making friends in each new port. In fact, she says she found that ''The world is a pretty nice place, and as long as you respect people, everybody's the same, and they're nice to you. Everybody was friendly.''

The real problem, she says, was that she was afraid to get too close to people, always knowing she'd have to leave. In fact many of her worst moments were ''having to leave places and be alone again after I'd just made new friends.'' That made lasting friendships, such as Olivier's, all the more valuable, she says.

Calling her voyage ''a crash course in life,'' Tania says she's glad she undertook it rather than going to college, and that she learned more from her firsthand experiences than from all the courses, lectures and textbooks she'd ever had in school. Besides practical matters, she learned about human nature, other cultures, the value of hard work and friendship, and the ability to reason things out, she says.

Her father agrees that the voyage was a success. "It turned out to be much better than we would have imagined in our wildest dreams," he says. "Tania got so much more. She has become a very accomplished person."

January, 1988

⚓

THE AGONY OF ANDREW

Survivors of Hurricane Andrew—the worst natural disaster in South Florida's history, which wrecked thousands of boats—tell their stories.

BY MICHAEL VERDON

August 24, 1992, is a day that will live in infamy in South Florida. It was the day that Hurricane Andrew ripped through Dade County at speeds of over 200 miles per hour, wrecking a half-dozen marinas, tearing up hundreds of docks, destroying thousands of boats. In just a few short hours, the worst natural disaster in the history of the Miami area caused an estimated billion dollars' worth of damage to the boating community—more than ten times the cost of Hurricanes Hugo and Bob combined.

For George Horak, Andrew is a name that brings on a shudder. The founder of the Miami Sailing club, his main concern two days before the storm hit was to preserve his fleet of thirty-three sailing vessels and the club's fifty-foot regatta motoryacht, *Tango*. Most of the boats were safe on land, but eight of the fleet and *Tango* were in adjoining slips at Dinner Key Marina.

The club had a contingency plan in case of hurricanes—tow the sailboats behind *Tango* to a hurricane hole on Key Biscayne. Unfortunately, only one other member of the club, Miguel Gutierrez, showed up to help Horak, which meant that the boats would have to stay in the marina. Working feverishly, the pair decided to sink the small sailboats in their slips in order to minimize structural damage. They would retrieve them after the hurricane had passed.

By early Sunday evening, they were finished. All day long, frantic boat owners had been coming and going to and from Dinner Key. Some had decided to anchor their boats outside in Biscayne Bay; others simply doubled the lines between their boats and the docks. No one had any intention of facing down the hurricane in their boat.

Except Horak. He had ridden out a three-day hurricane off the coast of Uruguay in 1963, and believed he had the experience to handle Andrew. He also felt that *Tango*, a wooden-hulled 1934 Casey yacht, had given too many years of service simply to be abandoned to the hurricane. It was a decision that not many yachtsmen would make— or agree with. But it was Horak's choice, and once he committed himself to it, he was prepared to see it through to the end—even if it meant gambling with his life.

At 11:00 PM, he fired up the boat's twin 453 GM diesels and headed toward the entrance to the harbor. Because his generator wasn't working, his only source of light was a small flashlight he carried with him in the cabin. This meant, in effect, that he would be working blind through the hurricane.

At the mouth of the harbor, he met his first obstacle of the night. "Someone had anchored out his boat and had tied a line across the entrance to the harbor," says Horak.

"But the line was just a few inches below the water's surface, so it was invisible."

The line fouled the starboard propeller, crippling *Tango*. Furious, Horak had no choice but to go in the water and try to cut the boat loose. With nothing but a knife in hand, he jumped overboard and blindly slashed at the line jamming the prop. After much effort, he was able to free the boat, but not without cost to himself. The layers of barnacles along *Tango*'s bottom had cut his arms and chest into bloody ribbons.

With the winds steadily increasing, Horak steered the boat toward Key Biscayne. "My intent was to find a spot with no other boats, so we could swing freely," he says. This he did in a small lagoon west of Bill Baggs Cape Florida State Park. Working quickly, he dropped a massive 150-pound yachtsman's anchor and 150 feet of anchor rode. Then he rushed around deck, securing whatever he could before the heaviest winds hit.

By 2:30 AM, the winds were up to 90 miles per hour and rising fast. "It was like walking on the wings of an airplane in flight," Horak recounts. "It got to the point where you had to crawl like a worm along the deck."

Taking to the pilothouse, Horak started the engines in order to steady the boat. Things went well until 4:30 AM. Then all hell broke loose. With 160-mile-per-hour winds slapping *Tango* back and forth like a helpless child, Horak was barely able to maintain steerage. Then the port engine died. This caused the boat to drag backward—straight toward a concrete wall. Shoving the starboard throttle forward, he fought hard against the onslaught, but the boat kept giving ground.

Horak then watched in horror as the window beside him began to bulge inward. Turning just in time to avoid the explosion, he felt splinters of glass lodge in his back like a thousand needles. Three more windows exploded in succession, and suddenly the pilothouse was no longer a sanctuary, but a howling tornado of wind, rain, and flying glass.

Horak thought then that the boat might sink. Instead, *Tango* came to rest against a sandy beach and a group of mangroves. There was nothing else he could do. He put on a wetsuit and a pair of flippers, and sat on the cabin sole, waiting for fate to take its course.

As it turned out, fate was kind to him. *Tango* lost several layers of paint and was scraped badly along the starboard side, just inches above the waterline. But the boat did not take on water, and hours later, it was able to limp on one engine back to Dinner Key.

"At one point," says Horak, "I wondered if I had done the right thing. After all, most of the owners had tied their boats up at the marina and hurried off for higher ground."

What he saw on the way back convinced Horak that he had indeed done the right thing. Biscayne Bay had become a wasteland of sunken boats, a field of broken dreams. Everywhere he looked was wreckage: dismasted sailboats, flying bridges of sportfishermen just visible above the water's surface, dinghies floating aimlessly out to sea.

The mangroves lining the shore had been buzzsawed in half, and though he didn't know it, most of the reefs to the South had been decimated. The tempest had caused more destruction than Miami had ever known.

When he arrived at the marina, he saw that Dinner Key had fared no better. Some boats were skewered on pilings; others were perched on land; yet others were sunk in black water that was saturated with fuel and oil. To Horak, the scene of destruction seemed almost surreal, a vision of the apocalypse.

But he had made it, and when he met a friend whose boat had also survived the wrath of Andrew, they embraced.

Tommy Vann and Gus Lorences were not as fortunate as Horak. With friend Stephen Suszek, they had opted to take *Leviathan*, their forty-eight-foot sportfisherman, out of Black Point Marina into what they thought would be a safer anchorage.

The three had been working to restore this boat for months, hoping to start a charter business. Lorences had recently earned his commercial captain's license and Vann was studying for his.

But *Leviathan* was uninsured. Instead of running the risk of losing the boat at sea or at the marina, they decided to ride it out at nearby Elliott Key. They tied up at the dock of a ranger station, bow into the wind, and prepared for the worst.

At 4 AM it came. The boat had been handling the 190-mile-per-hour winds fairly well until the wind direction abruptly shifted to the north. When this happened, the ranger station splintered into a hundred different pieces, sending heavy wooden boards flying across *Leviathan*. When the boat's transom door came unhinged and started flapping wildly in the wind, the three decided to leave the cabin and venture out to the cockpit to secure it.

It was a mistake that would cost two of them their lives. Lorences was caught by the wind and immediately blown overboard, lost at sea. Almost simultaneously, a two-by-six plank shot across the boat through the darkness, decapitating Vann.

The boat then lurched sideways and angled up against the dock, flooding the cockpit. Suszek grabbed Vann's lifeless body, but abruptly let go when he realized he might be washed overboard. He climbed up into a large fish box, clung to the base of the tuna tower, and waited out the storm. The Coast Guard rescued him by helicopter the following afternoon. Vann's body was recovered five days later. Lorences is still missing, presumed dead.

After the initial shock passed, the boating community began to count casualties. It did not look good. Although loss of life was kept to a minimum, marinas from Dinner Key to Key Biscayne and all the way down to Black Point Marina—where a dry-stack storage facility collapsed, crushing hundreds of boats in one blow—were severely damaged. Private yacht clubs like Miami's Coral Reef were flooded by Andrew's surge. Many owners had no idea where their boats were for weeks after the hurricane, since many boats had either sunk or floated ashore.

Though the tally will probably never be complete, it is estimated that 2,000 boats either sank or were crippled beyond repair, and countless others sustained some damage. Many of these were big boats, in the fifty- to sixty-foot range, which pushed the total damage in dollars upward. Frank Herhold, executive director of the Marine Industries Association of South Florida, estimates that $600 million to $700 million was lost in boats alone. That, combined with marina damage, businesses destroyed, and loss of potential income, adds up to a final bill of as much as a billion dollars for South Florida's boating community.

November, 1992

⚓

ROUGH PASSAGE

What begins as a simple delivery trip to Bermuda turns into a nightmare as one thing after another on the thirty-seven-foot sailboat goes seriously wrong.

BY HANK HALSTED

Delivery captains don't have much choice—the owner needs his boat sailed from here to there, and you either take the job or you don't. Usually, times being what they are, you take it.

Last November 25, my handpicked crew and I arrived in Wilmington, Delaware, and were met by Eric Rosenfeld, owner of the new thirty-seven-foot sloop *High Beta*. He needed the boat delivered to Bermuda and then St. Martin, where it would become part of a new bareboat charter fleet.

During the drive to the yard in Delaware City, through early winter rain and wind, I thought to ask the meaning of the yacht's name. Rosenfeld, a professor of finance at Harvard, explained, "In elite financial circles, 'high beta' is the term placed on extremely high-risk ventures."

Had I been more prescient, I would have taken this foreshadowing to heart.

Aboard the boat, we immediately donned warm clothes and oilskins to begin our survey of the yacht. *High Beta* was a high-aspect-ratio sloop with fin keel and skeg rudder, generally a very light and fast design. Aside from some mottled fiberglasswork in the stem and the peculiarly high position of the manual bilge pump strainer, she checked out quite well.

Having become relatively well acquainted as we performed our go-to-sea chores, the four of us felt we had the makings of a good team. Kurt was a very successful one-design sailboat racer currently working with a major marine supply house in Philadelphia. Although a bit highstrung and lacking in extensive bluewater experience, he had good knowledge of boats, hardware, and helmsmanship. Jane had cruised with her parents out of Newport, Rhode Island, and had done some coastal deliveries. Matt and I had been friends for many years. A lifetime sailor, he'd been a boatyard mechanic for ten years and coowner of a New England yard for the previous four. His knowledge of seamanship and engineering as well as his sense of humor would prove invaluable in the forthcoming voyage. I, who had covered 70,000 miles racing yachts and making deliveries, by my reckoning, was captain and navigator.

Having made many trips to the Caribbean, I knew the chemistry of crew relationships could make or break a passage. We seemed to have the proper formula on *High Beta* and I was pleased.

At 1:30 AM, a cold front passed, leaving clear skies and a cold, brisk northwesterly breeze. In these conditions our shakedown cruise to Cape May, New Jersey, was uneventful. We arrived just after noon and the rest of the day became a blur of mast-tuning; making repairs; taking on water, ice, fuel, and provisions; installing life-harness deck lines; and changing engine oil and filters. It was well after dark before the yacht was thoroughly prepared.

At 5:00 the following morning we got under way. It was a frigid early winter morning, the temperature in the low twenties, but crystal clear with a blustery northwesterly breeze. Outside the breakwater we set a double-reefed mainsail and working jib, and we had fine downwind sailing. *High Beta* was handling beautifully and beginning to surf on the building seas. She could well have carried more sail but we were treating her gently as we got to know her. Even so we averaged an easy 7 knots of speed.

By 11:00 the sun was high enough to take some of the chill out of the Force 5 northwester. Kurt came on deck and said he hadn't been able to sleep very well. At first he thought it was Matt's snoring but later realized that the automatic bilge pump had been going on and off intermittently. I pondered this for a short time, then called below to Matt and asked him if he would turn the pump off so we could ascertain whether or not we had a substantial leak.

By noon the bilge water had risen slightly and we turned on the pump to remove it. Nothing happened. The very reputable-brand pump that had given us thirty-six hours of perfect service had burned out. This didn't make me particularly happy, but we still had the lesser-capacity shower sump pump and the manual bilge pump. The most suspicious area for leakage was the mottled glasswork in the stem. We found it to be weeping a little but hardly enough to cause worry, and so continued on our way.

Jane had just come on watch at 4:00 when a resounding crash shook the entire boat. The mainsheet tore loose from the boom, and the boom came to rest against the starboard lower shroud. Nobody needed to call me, nor did I need to use the companionway steps—I took the adrenaline highway. A quick inspection revealed the problem, caused by a bolt that had never been properly tightened. The repair was simple.

We completed this task just as we were crossing the wake of a large Japanese fishing vessel. The helpful communications officer gave us a position fix and wished us luck in our race to the Gulf Stream against the forthcoming low-pressure system. Toward the end of our transmission, reception began to break up as it became quite evident that our deck-mounted antenna was ineffective in the troughs of the waves.

More water had accumulated in the bilge by this time, and we rigged the shower sump as a bilge pump. Only a true cynic would find humor in the fact that our very reputable-brand sump pump gave us perfect service for twelve and a half minutes and then burned out as well. Amid many jokes about the merits of buckets and muscle as opposed to electronics, we bailed the boat dry. We only had about fifteen to twenty gallons to remove and it didn't take long. But we were beginning to wonder about this increasingly high-beta venture.

Wednesday evening brought more exquisite sailing conditions and, much to our delight, a warming trend as the northwesterly breeze abated. I was grateful for the forty-degree temperatures, but not without mixed emotions as our speed dropped from 8 knots to 6. Although biting cold, the northwester had helped us put many miles of ocean between ourselves and Cape May in a short time.

Also, surfing off the six- to eight-foot seas had been exciting and good fun.

At midnight, we shook out the reefs in the mainsail and gradually trimmed sails through the night as the warming breeze worked around into the northeast. Dawn the next day was a vibrant kaleidoscopic sunrise created by a partial layer of broken cumulus to the east. *High Beta* came to life close-reaching.

At 9:00 I was at the helm when suddenly a cracking noise resounded deep in the bilges. It was the most ominous sound I'd ever heard aboard a boat. Instantly an electrifying chill ran down my back. Kurt took the helm while Matt and I searched the bilges for damage. We knew it hadn't been the noise of a collision, but was something structural. And yet there was no visible damage. We warily shrugged it off.

I returned to the helm and everyone else, since they were at this point wide awake, went about various tasks. Jane began stuffing the Thanksgiving turkey. Matt cleaned up and Kurt continued snooping around the bilges. It wasn't a minute later that Matt came back on deck foaming toothpaste, lecturing me on the negative aspects of taking coastal cruisers to sea. His tirade lasted several minutes before he let me know that the freshwater pressure was not working.

Just as he repaired the faulty wiring on the freshwater pump, Jane asked him for help lighting the oven. He tried several times, gave me an icy glare, went forward to get the tool kit, then began dismantling the oven. I chuckled, "Happy Thanksgiving."

After an hour, the oven was lit and the turkey baking. But we weren't able to get the temperature above 165 degrees, even with the oven door taped closed. There was nothing to do but let the turkey sit forever and see what happened.

Having completed this repair stint, Matt came on deck to relieve me at the helm. He was grateful for the change. I remained in the cockpit and we exchanged sporadic conversation, mostly with regard to the uncanny number of repairs we'd had to make. Our last exchange as I went below was in reference to the barometer, which hadn't moved from 29.9 inches since we'd come aboard.

"What do you think of the barometer?"

"What barometer?"

"Yeah, you're right. Must be just a picture of one."

Through the rest of the morning the breeze continued to clock around to the southeast. At 2:00 PM we entered the Gulf Stream, tacked east, and started the engine to help keep our speed up, hoping to minimize our time in the Stream. At 4:00, as we were approaching the Stream's axis, Matt took the helm. Shortly thereafter we were all snapped to attention once again by an ominous crack. This one shook the stern section of the boat. Again we looked for damage, but could find none. Perhaps we had hit something with the rudder, but it still seemed to work just fine. Again, we tried to shrug it off. But we had, in truth, been set on edge.

By 8:00 we had accumulated a lot of water in the bilge. Its sloshing about was unnerving as we ran off to level the boat so we could bail. More than an hour was needed to dry the bilges this time, filling the bucket with teacups and dumping it into the cockpit to drain. It was exhausting work and somewhat nauseating, staring at the water as it surged from side to side. We set up a rotating system with two people bailing while the other two steered and rested. After removing about 75 gallons we

searched the boat everywhere for leaks. We didn't seem
to be taking water aft, as there was no water washing
forward around the engine. The fiberglasswork around the
ribs and keel bolts was solid. We decided to check the
small leak in the stem. Matt went head-first, then I
handed him a knife and he scraped away the mottled
fiberglass. "Hey Hank—I can see the running light right
through the stem!"

"Great! Want some epoxy?"

"Yeah, and maybe some of those Handi-Wipes."

As I passed them forward, I reflected on how fortunate
we were to have this two-part underwater epoxy along.
This was the first delivery on which I'd carried it. Pres-
ently, Matt emerged. "That's good stuff, and the Handi-
Wipes make good cloth. I think it'll hold."

It was 10:00 and my watch when we finally got under
way. Everyone else went instantly to sleep, exhausted by
the ordeal. I'd been on deck for awhile when I remembered the turkey. Oh Lord! It had been in the oven more
than 12 hours! I quickly surveyed the horizon, locked the
wheel and dashed below. Tearing at the tape, I pulled the
oven door open and then extracted the beast. It didn't
look bad. The skin, although somewhat dry and crunchy,
was golden brown and beneath that parched exterior was
some of the most succulent turkey I'd ever eaten. I quickly
made a sandwich and returned to the helm, happily con-
founded. At least something good had arisen from our
calamities.

At midnight my watch was officially over. I decided to
keep on for another hour to let the others rest. I found
myself in the sobering situation where the captain is required to parcel out the strength of his crew. Also, I
needed time to think. I could hear water again under the

cabin sole. Where was it coming from? Mentally I went over and over the boat. When Matt came on deck at 1:00 AM, I had settled on the stuffing box or rudder configuration in the stern. It had to be there.

I dug everything out of the lazarette and sail locker, then took the light and dove into the stern cavity. As my light illuminated it that same electric chill ran down my back. The entire steering system had dropped out of its mountings, leaving the upper end of the rudder post unsupported. Every time we punched a wave or steered off another, the rudder post and the quadrant, which holds the steering cables, would rock 30 degrees side to side, radically flexing the stern section and tearing at the glasswork around the stuffing box.

This meant trouble. Now we had no sarcastic one-liners. Within two minutes the sails were down and we'd hove to. No words were spoken and none were needed as Matt and I made a jury-rigged repair and together we hauled the 220-pound rudder system back into position and tied it off.

As we worked, we discovered another leak at the through-hull fitting for the starboard scupper. More Handi-Wipes. More epoxy. A bit more cursing, too.

We had been completely preoccupied with emergency repairs for about an hour before I had time to take stock of the situation. Conditions had built to a Force 5 to Force 6 southeaster. The boat was pitching about considerably as we lay ahull. We had two fried bilge pumps. The manual bilge pump was functional; however, the suction device hung level with the engine, not deep in the bilge. Thus, even though the cabin sole was completely awash, the pump strainer had yet to get wet.

It was then that I noticed Kurt. He was wandering

about, somewhat dazed and obviously quite frightened, murmuring about wanting to get off. He was in a mild state of nervous shock, and hardly to be blamed. For a man who'd never been far offshore he was witnessing a scary situation. I did my best to calm him but to no avail; he wasn't rational. Fortunately the medical kit was complete and I gave him ten milligrams of Valium to keep him calm and away from the EPIRB.

With Kurt safely below, I quickly took Jane aside and asked her to put together a ditch kit. The very real possibility of abandonment had arisen and it was time to have all our emergency gear in one handy spot. She gathered our strobes, life jackets, a flashlight, emergency water, some canned food, the EPIRB, my sextant, and put them in the quarterberth. She accomplished all this surreptitiously so that Kurt wouldn't notice. Ah, Jane. She was solid as a rock, showing only efficiency and no fear.

In the meantime, Matt had been tearing the head apart gathering enough hose to rig the manual pump properly. I clipped on my safety line and went forward to clear the working jib off the deck and rig the storm jib. As I finished, Matt had the pump working.

We pumped and cleaned the boat up somewhat, then at 4:00 set the double-reefed mainsail and storm jib. It was good to be on our way again. Matt steered and I manned the pump.

By 6:00 I began to get tired and awakened Jane to operate the pump. Conditions at this point were a solid Force 6. In order to be immediately available, I huddled in the leeward side of the cockpit trying to sleep. Although physically and mentally exhausted from the hours of constant repairs and worry, I doubt I slept at all. Between the pounding motion, the wind, sporadic dowsings, and my concern for the boat, I was kept just this side of a decent doze.

At 8:30 Jane went below and sent Kurt up to relieve her at the pump. I took the helm to allow Matt some relief. Through the morning the weather continued to build, approaching a Force 8 full-gale southeaster. As we pressed on with Matt and me steering and Kurt and Jane alternately pumping and napping, I continued to be impressed with the handling characteristics of this responsive boat while going to weather in a rough seaway. It was a paradoxical shame that she'd literally fallen apart in relatively calm seas and now handled like a dream in the rough stuff.

Fatigue, especially for Matt and myself, was becoming a very real consideration, however.

At noon I took the helm and immediately noticed that the boat was beginning to handle sluggishly. Even with our constant pumping she had become heavy. Water was sufficiently high over the cabin sole for us to bail using the bucket out the companionway. And still we seemed to be losing. At this point I began to wonder when I would be justified in tearing the man's boat apart, smashing out bunks, cabinets, and the one-piece cabin sole in order to find the leak. Where was it?!

At 1:10 the upper bushing that held the rudder post fell out again and we hove to for repairs. Sails in, I started the engine. At full cruising throttle I could barely keep the boat head to wind, occasionally being blown right around through 180 degrees. Again we replaced the bushing, this time tying it in place with marlin.

With the boat level we were able to see that the water as well over the floorboards, approaching the engine and batteries. Using more hose pilfered from the head we rigged the engine raw-water intakes as an additional bilge pump. After three hours of frenzied manual pumping plus an additional 100 gallons removed by the engine, water level was again below the cabin sole.

At 4:00 we left Jane at the helm just keeping the boat head to wind while Matt and I hit the sodden bunks, exhausted. Thirty-five minutes later Kurt awakened me, very excited. He had found a surging leak through the forward port keelbolt. We had to break the wooden collar from around the mast where it went through the cabin sole in order to properly get at the leakage, but inspection revealed that Kurt was right. A steady and forceful jet of water was shooting into the boat. Hallelujah! It could be fixed.

Another exhausting hour of pumping had the boat almost dry. And the leakage, from this area, was all but stopped. By now the wind had worked around to the south. The full-gale conditions continued but I knew from this most recent shift that it would be only a matter of hours before the wind finished clocking into the northwest. It would blow, and blow very hard, for a few days to come. But it would blow from behind us. That prospect was heartening.

At 1:00 the following morning, the wind finally blasted out of the northwest. We set the storm jib and were on our way. At 9:45 AM, I had just awakened from a glorious few hours of alpha-level sleep. Matt and I were sipping coffee, ankles awash, marveling at how blasé we'd become toward the circumstances that might have caused soaring blood pressure.

As if to test this premise, Kurt suddenly shouted from the cockpit that the rudder bushing had fallen out again and the post was really rocking. I couldn't believe it. "Not again! OK, I'll have a look. Do your best to steer gently."

The rudder in this thirty-seven-foot sloop is hung from a box underneath the fiberglass cockpit sole. Our jury rig had the rudder hanging in its proper position, centered in the box. There is a false bottom to the box also, about two inches below the original, which supports the bushing for the rudder. Burrowing back through the lazarette, I expected to find that the bushing had again slid.

I was greeted by another awesome surprise. Yes, the rudder post was loose, rocking, and again overstressing the stern section. But it wasn't the bushing this time. The entire false bottom had torn free from the mounting box. There was no longer any way to reset the bushing, and no longer a way to stop the rudder's motion from tearing at the stern section. We were 291 miles from St. Georges, Bermuda, and rather needed to steer.

Back in the cockpit, I shrugged. What can you do when you can do nothing? I asked Kurt to steer as little as possible, permitting the boat to swing through arcs of 60 degrees if necessary as she careened off the eight- to fifteen-foot seas.

Every hour I checked the stern section for damage. It seemed to hold up okay for a couple of hours, but at 1:00 PM I knew we had to stop. A small area of glasswork on the starboard side, exactly at waterline level, was alternately bubbling then moistening as we rolled. The fiberglass was delaminating! I emerged wearing my best poker face and asked Kurt to heave to . . . gently.

I summoned Matt to the lazarette for a summit conference. He agreed that the rudder was tearing the boat apart. After racking my brain, the only solution I could find was to let it go—lower the rudder right out of the boat, plug the stuffing hole and haul the rudder back aboard if possible. We could fabricate a sweep-rudder out of the spinnaker pole and floorboards. It would be no fun to steer that rig for 275 miles downwind in a North Atlantic winter gale, but it was our most viable option.

I was mentally engineering, when Matt called from the lazarette. He had another idea. To this day, I can't tell you exactly how he did it, but using the old bushing, broken fiberglass pieces, $5/16$-inch Dacron line, string, and underwater epoxy, Matt reset the bushing inside the ruddermount box. The repair was nothing short of a genius feat.

It took until evening for the epoxy to harden thoroughly. Apprehensively we turned the wheel, very carefully at first, then more vigorously as it seemed to hold. Again, hooray! Again we would set off under sail. Again . . . for how long this time?

Through the evening the rudder seemed to work fine. At 8:30 intermittent lines of very heavy squalls began shrieking past. Several times during the night the wind gusted more than 60 knots, pegging the anemometer. The seas built to twelve to twenty feet. Steering, regardless of the structural integrity of the system, became quite a chore. The horizon obscured by the inky blackness, we had only the compass and the occasional roar of a crashing wave by which to orient ourselves. Once more, very exciting sailing. And the rudder held.

The next day dawned with a thin overcast between the squalls. The large seas came in sets, some truly immense. Trying to baby the steering system continued to be an interesting game as we fell off some of the big ones, surfing occasionally to 14¾ knots on the toppling effervescent walls.

At 6:30 PM we completed our first twenty-four-hour day

of the voyage during which it wasn't necessary to heave to or alter course for repairs. The weather and seas had abated to the northwest, Force 5, and *High Beta* continued to sail well with the storm jib and double-reefed main. Occasional pumping kept the leakage below floorboard level and out of sight, if not out of mind.

There was one puzzle left for Matt, though. At 11:00 the following morning, the engine stopped. We shared a moment of silence as the thought of losing our bottom-line pump passed simultaneously through all our minds. It took only a moment, though, for our mechanical mentor to locate the loose wire in the electrical fuel pump.

There was a puzzle for me also when the loran stopped working while I was doing my landfall calculations at 4:00. Twilight was an hour away and two-thirds of the sky was overcast. We turned the boat around and had an interesting race with the clouds until twilight, at which time I was able to get a good fix by stars Altair, Vega, and Kochab. St. Georges was seventy-eight miles south-southeast, the sea was smooth, and our spirits were high.

At dawn as we approached North Rock, I sounded reveille, then we all got busy cleaning up the incredible mess that had accumulated during the fiasco. Eric Rosenfeld was waiting for us at St. Georges and I figured that a very clean boat would help to ease the impact of the bad news we had for him.

September, 1981

⚓

SCHOOL OF HARD KNOCKS

The Canadian Coast Guard holds Rigid Hull Inflatable Operator Training School in the roughest waters it can find. Wimps need not apply.

BY LOUISA RUDEEN

The art of "station-keeping" involves keeping your boat within two boatlengths of the same position, no matter how rough the conditions. As waves battered the ship-killing crags of Cape Beale, British Columbia, my instructor worked the gears and throttles of our Zodiac to hold us so close to the rocks that I couldn't bear to look at them.

"Now you try it," he said.

Wimping out was not an option.

The time for that would have been weeks before, when the president of Zodiac of North America, J. J. Marie, and I were (naturally) discussing inflatables. He surprised me by saying that Zodiacs are used regularly by the Navy SEALs and other military and paramilitary organizations for dangerous missions. And I'd always thought of "rubber boats" as innocuous tenders.

To illustrate his point, he told me about what sounded like "riot school"—the Canadian Coast Guard's RHIOT School, short for Rigid Hull Inflatable Operator Training. This hands-on course trains Search and Rescue (SAR) workers to handle Zodiac Hurricane rigid-hull inflatables (RHIs) in extreme conditions. He said that the school is held in winter only, in Bamfield, British Columbia, on the wild Pacific Coast of Vancouver Island—just so the seas will be as nasty as possible.

How could I resist?

The Canadian Coast Guard graciously granted my request to drop in on a RHIOT School session. So one morning in early March, I found myself driving down an unpaved logging road complete with logging trucks piled high with former fir trees. I learned that if you see one of these vehicles barreling down on you, it's best to pull off the road—fast.

Bamfield was worth the drive. A peaceful fishing resort that serves as the gateway to the abundant waters of Barkley Sound and its protected Broken Group of islets, the town exists on, for, and by the water. In fact, you have to travel by boat across Bamfield Inlet to get from one side of town to the other. (One morning I was charmed to see a young boy on his way to school by Boston Whaler, his golden retriever in the bow.)

RHIOT School is held at the Bamfield Coast Guard Lifeboat Station at the mouth of the inlet, which allows its own SAR crew rapid access to the sound and the Pacific Ocean beyond, past the forbidding rocks of Cape Beale. The station's assets include a forty-four-foot motor lifeboat, a twenty-four-foot Zodiac Hurricane 733 powered by twin 150-horsepower Mariner outboards, and several nineteen-foot Zodiac Hurricane 590s, powered by twin 90-horsepower Mariners.

These RHIs, manufactured in Richmond, British Columbia, have deep-V fiberglass hulls fitted with multichambered inflatable tubes. Each is custom-rigged with motorcycle-style seats for secure riding in rough seas, weatherproof instrument consoles, a tow post, and an arch that holds a self-righting system (more on that later).

The Coast Guard uses RHIs because of their unique attributes: fendering, buoyancy, and stability, coupled with fast, deep-V performance. You can take an RHI alongside another boat without harming it. In waves and surf, the tube buoys up the hill and the motors evenly, preventing the boat from being swamped. The tube also absorbs most of the shocks caused by impact with rough seas. And rough water is where most SAR situations occur. "It might be blowing 40 knots and raining, but we still have to go out and do our jobs," says Kevin Tomsett, one of the RHIOT School's founders.

The five-day course followed a rigorous format. Mornings, starting at 0800 hours, were devoted to classroom work, held in an upstairs room of the Bamfield Station swept by icy March breezes that blew in through an open door. Instructor Bill Mather's Dickensian philosophy prescribed cold air and strong coffee to keep us from nodding off.

That was hardly likely, as the lectures given by Mather and fellow instructors Dave Christney and Cam Murray on such topics as search methods, wave dynamics, and rough-water boat handling were fascinating, and the chalkboard-talks that prepared us for the on-water exercises we would do each afternoon were crucial to our continued well-being.

At 1300 hours each day we headed for the locker rooms and squirmed into our protective gear. The first layer was a one-piece polypropylene inner-liner, soft as a child's pajamas, followed by a "drysuit" with neoprene seals at the ankles, wrists and neck. The drysuit drill was to put it on, then hold the neck seal slightly open, squat down and press your arms to our sides. This forced the air out of the suit and gave it a watertight seal with your skin. On shore, I found this bulky getup to be a bit ridiculous, but on the boat its flexibility and warmth overcame my objections. In addition, we wore sea boots, helmets, PFDs, and Coast Guard-issue Oakley wraparound sunglasses. We looked like a small tactical unit of space aliens.

Before I joined the class, the other students had already practiced basic RHI boat handling and towing. My first exercise on the water was to be "pacing." This tricky discipline involves approaching a moving boat with your Zodiac, matching your speed to the boat's, then pulling alongside so your tube touches its hull. This skill can be crucial in a medical emergency—for example, when someone out boating alone has a heart attack while under way. It's also used in some law-enforcement boarding situations.

On a cloudy, raw afternoon, the Bamfield station's forty-four-foot lifeboat began steaming up and down Trevor Channel in Barkley Sound at a steady pace of 7 knots. Tomsett, who was on board a Hurricane 590 with me, demonstrated the maneuver first, neatly inserting the RHI between the lifeboat's bow and stern wakes, then pulling alongside it so swiftly it seemed like we had added "sideways" to the gears along with forward and reverse. Ever so gently, he nudged the tube into the side of the lifeboat.

Then it was my turn. With my heart in my throat, I took the controls. On my first attempt (as well as my second and third), I was repelled by the lifeboat's bow wake, overcorrected my steering so much it looked like I was doing the watusi, dithered three feet from the lifeboat, then finally slammed the inflatable right into its side and bounced off.

Eventually, I got the knack, and was able to pace the boat and pull alongside it with such confidence that photographer Dan Nerney, who had accompanied me here, could safely transfer himself and his camera equipment from the lifeboat to the RHI.

Then, the lifeboat sped up to 10 knots, its wake dynamics changed, and I had to learn the drill all over again.

When all the students had mastered the technique, we moved into rougher water around craggy Whittlestone Point, near Cape Beale. Here waves were rolling onto rocks and boulders, refracting around them, reflecting off them, and generally creating turbulent conditions.

In the middle of this maelstrom, our instructors expected us to keep our boats still. Station-keeping is a critical skill for the driver of a Coast Guard Zodiac to have when there's a rescue swimmer on shore, attached to his RHI by a long tether. As Mather had pointed out in his chalkboard talk that morning, "You can't leave him."

The secret of station-keeping involves choosing a reference point on land and working the throttles gently but effectively to keep the boat at the same position relative to it. The RHI's buoyancy and stability make the task much easier than it would be in a standard deep-V boat, but it's still no walk in the park—especially when your reference point is a very close, very tall and very sharp rock.

The next afternoon, the lesson was rough-water boat handling, taught atop eight- to ten-foot rollers—Pacific waves piling up at the mouth of shallower Barkley Sound. First we learned how to approach a body floating in the water and bring it into the boat. "Oscar," a dummy in a bright orange PFD, gave a performance worthy of his name.

Then we rode the waves. Driving the 590 at about 30 miles per hour (top end is 38 miles per hour), I tackled head seas, beam seas, and following seas. In a nineteen-foot inflatable on the back of a ten-foot swell, I was gripped by the sensation of just how insignificant we are on the face of the ocean.

Still, I had horsepower on my side. Tomsett taught me how to look for low spots in head seas and drive quickly through them. But not with *too* much throttle, or the boat would take flight. While the instructors allowed us occasionally to test the edge of the envelope by leaping free of the sea, as Mather put it, "You've got no control if the props are out of the water."

"Look for a window in the waves," Tomsett said as we ran along in the trough between beam seas. I practiced staying on the backs of swells, accelerating from one to the next through the calmer spots or "windows." Following seas were the worst, because of the danger of "stuffing" the bow. Again, the trick was to ride on the back of a wave. But when one launched me down its face, threatening to stuff me into its brother, I would trim up to lift the bow, and power up to stay in control. Each time, after a knuckle-biting downhill ride, the bow would gently climb the back of the next wave. Again and again, I was amazed by how much punishment the inflatable tube absorbed.

Finally we ran home, tired but triumphant, noticing for the first time all day the beauty of the island-studded sound, in summer a favorite of fishermen, boaters, and kayakers from all over the Northwest. Lazily, seabirds wheeled above the cold, clear water.

The next morning I was in that water, nervously anticipating the first icy drip that would penetrate my drysuit (none did). We were simulating a capsize, something that rarely happens to RHIs, thanks to the tube's inherent buoyancy—but could, in extreme conditions. The instructors used a crane to flip one of the 590s at the Coast Guard station dock. Then, led by Cam Murray, a group of students and I swam over and ducked under the upside-down RHI to see what the cockpit looked like inverted. It was surprisingly bright in there.

We swam back out, deployed a safety line from the boat's transom, and hung onto it while Murray pulled the trigger of the self-righting system, custom-installed by Zodiac Hurricane. This opened the valve on a CO_2 tank on the boat's transom, which filled the airbag attached to the radar arch. Slowly, but inexorably, we saw one of the tubes rise into the air; then the boat popped free of the water and landed, with a splash, on its feet again.

The versatile, almost magical rigid-hull inflatable had surprised me once again. Never again, after surviving RHIOT School, will I dismiss it as merely a wimpy tender. It is a tool that helps Coast Guard SAR workers save lives in extreme conditions—while staying alive themselves.

June, 1994

⚓

A RIDE ON THE WILD SIDE

Heavy fog and high seas punish seven speedboats racing from San Francisco to Los Angeles.

BY PETER A. JANSSEN

Above all, the fog. Thick, swirling, wet San Francisco fog. So heavy that when the race started, just off the St. Francis Yacht Club, we couldn't see the Golden Gate Bridge. So heavy, in fact, that we could barely see the outlines of the six other speedboats next to us, all lined up for a two-day, bone-numbing race to Los Angeles— 423 miles away.

A few minutes before we started, the other drivers asked Betty Cook, a former world champion who knows the California coast, how to take the bridge, since we couldn't see it. "Head for the south tower," she said. "If you go to the south side of the tower you could save a few seconds, but the surge will probably push you onto the rocks. So take the north side of the tower, but don't go too far north or you'll be in the commercial shipping lane."

As we hurtled through the fog at 55 miles per hour, all

that became irrelevant. We didn't even see the south tower until we were twenty yards away. Then our driver, Karl Koster, who has been racing on the West Coast since he was eleven years old, swung the wheel of our Cigarette 35 over quickly so we skipped around the north side, almost within touching distance.

So far, so good, except that our loran went out before we passed under the bridge and did not come on again until we came off plane at the mandatory refueling stop in Monterey, ninety-five miles down the coast. We didn't see any of the other race boats. Betty Cook, however, driving a Formula 30, and Dick Genth, driving a Chris-Craft 31, bumped each other in the murk just beyond the bridge.

A few miles out, our eyes straining ahead while we hoped desperately that we wouldn't see anything, we closed fast—very fast—on a big sloop ghosting along under power, broadside to us. At the last second Koster swerved across its bow.

Then the Pacific itself. As we left San Francisco Bay, we slammed into six- to eight-foot seas; not choppy waves, like the Atlantic, but long rollers with an occasional cross chop just to keep you awake. Flying low in the Cigarette, we'd come off the top of a roller and freefall until the boat hit the trough seconds later. It felt like jumping off a ladder onto a concrete floor every few seconds—except that the floor was moving forward at 55 miles an hour.

These rollers seemed disjointed; they were not part of a wave family, they had no pattern. Usually on a speedboat you can work into the rhythm of the waves, even when you're taking a pounding. Your body can get into the flow of the up-and-down motion, much like tuning into the rhythm of a hill when you're skiing down a series of moguls. But not here—only drop, pound, then pound some more. Sometimes there wouldn't even be another roller after the fall and, totally unexpectedly, you'd fall once only to hesitate for a fraction of a second and then fall again.

Being on a boat, hanging on as tight as humanly possible, was like being inside a cocoon. The roar of the twin engines changed, after a few minutes, into a steady ringing inside my race helmet; it sounded like a fire alarm going off a block or so away. There was no life outside the boat, only the rush of wind and water, the sensation of flat-out speed. Your entire existence became enveloped in the cockpit of the Cigarette; there was no room—no thinking or feeling space left—for anything else. Every ounce of energy, every instinct for self-preservation, was focused entirely on that spot in time. All that mattered was the speed, the pounding, the wind, the noise, the fog—all wrapped up in a thirty-five-foot boat hurtling down the west side of the continent.

This clearly was no casual speedboat race. Long planned by Southern California industrialist Bob Nordskog, himself a veteran offshore racer, it involved many of the nation's leading boat manufacturers, and was designed both as a fund-raiser for the Olympics and as a vehicle to promote powerboating on the West Coast. To enter, each manufacturer had to write a $25,000 check to the U.S. Olympic Committee; each boat had to be a production-line, off-the-shelf stock V-hull, one that boating enthusiasts as well as professional racers could use and enjoy. In addition, each boat was powered by identical MerCruiser 370 engines with TRS drives—again, a standard engine for real people.

Since the power plants were equal, each manufacturer

had a great deal of prestige tied up in how well his hull performed. And the industry leaders had showed up in force. Dick Genth, driving the Chris-Craft, had spent many years racing offshore; he was also president of the company. In the cockpit with him was Ernest Schmidt, a Chris-Craft vice president, on his first offshore race. Betty Cook drove the Formula with her racing throttleman John Connor, but Formula Vice President Scott Porter was also on board. Reggie Fountain, who drove the thirty-three-foot Fountain Executioner *Perfect 10,* was not only a champion racer, he was also president of Fountain Powerboats. Wellcraft President Bob Long, Cobalt President Pack St. Clair, and Baja President Doug Smith were aboard their companies' entries. Koster, a San Jose boat wholesaler, drove our Cigarette 35, but also on board were Cigarette President Kees Sanders; Bill Helfrick, a San Jose accountant (and expert navigator); Jerry Berton, *MB&S*'s high performance editor, and me.

The course: 95 miles from San Francisco to Monterey for mandatory refueling, then 117 miles to Morro Bay for an overnight stop. The next morning, 106 miles around both Point Arguello and Point Conception—some of the roughest water off the U.S.—to Santa Barbara for another mandatory refueling, and then flat out for the final leg of 105 miles to Long Beach with the finish line off the stern of the Queen Mary.

Back in the office in New York, the race had seemed like a piece of cake. After all, 423 miles in four legs in a 60-plus-mile-an-hour speedboat—how hard can that be? Once we started gathering in San Francisco, however, we had second, third, and fourth thoughts.

For openers, the day before the race the wind was howling through at 21 knots, with six- to eight-foot seas.

Betty Cook took her Formula out for a trial run beyond the bridge and came back shaking her head. "The water's rough out there," she reported. Then Reggie Fountain went out and back. "I couldn't see a thing," he said.

The pre-race drivers' meeting did little to calm the mounting unease. "Remember that you'll be in a following sea," advised Nordskog. "Don't put the bow through the next wave, and don't take water over the transom. Otherwise you'll be safe. And if the seas get to the fifteen-foot range, we'll call it off."

Koster and I looked at each other quickly. *Fifteen feet?*

Then Nordskog asked if there were any questions, and Ernie Schmidt raised his hand. "Can we start in Santa Barbara?"

That night at dinner, the fog started rolling in. And later, as I tried to sleep in my hotel room in Pacific Heights, all I could hear—all night, it seemed—was the echoing, forlorn two-tone boom of the foghorns. I was born and raised in San Francisco, and I remember lying in bed as a child, peacefully falling asleep while listening to the same sound. For me, the foghorns have always meant home; I'm back where I belong. But not that night. I was out of bed and dressed long before the five o'clock wakeup call from the hotel operator.

We were supposed to have another drivers' meeting at 6:20. Down on the dock, Betty was shaking her head as she wiped off the deck of her boat. Dick Genth was zipping up his white jumpsuit. "How'd you sleep?" I asked conversationally. "Sleep, hell," he replied. "I may throw up one more time." Karl Koster looked serious, and kept passing out Rolaids.

Nordskog postponed the start for half an hour, then fifteen minutes, then—although the fog didn't seem to be getting any better—we were off, thankful at least finally to be on our way. And after that the fog, the pounding, the Pacific flashing by, all the way to Monterey.

At the fuel dock there we looked at the boat; we had been hitting the water so hard that our race number—#1—was peeling off the bow. Genth, who put in twenty-two years as an Air Force fighter pilot before he even got started in the boat business, stood on the dock with his hands on his hips. "I'm waiting for the fun to begin," he said. "I haven't had any fun yet. That fog. . . ."

A subdued Reggie Fountain stared at the water. "I've got to tell you, I got some religion out there," he said, and he, too, shook his head.

That afternoon, on the second leg from Monterey to Morro Bay, the pounding took its toll. Boats started breaking down, falling out of the race. Betty Cook broke down about three miles off Big Sur, surely one of the most forbidding coastlines in the United States with its pounding surf and sheer cliffs. For more than two hours she was dead in the water, talking to her chopper overhead on her VHF—but, except for a few brief breaks in the fog, they couldn't see each other. The chopper pilot tried to direct a chase boat to help her, but the fog was too thick.

Her boat started taking on water. "We were about five minutes from breaking out the raft," she said, until John Connor got one engine going. Still all alone, Betty Cook and her crew limped into Morro Bay just as dusk was darkening to night.

For our part, we kept pounding on, the Cigarette cutting through the waves. We passed some whales and a shark—and almost lost Berton over the side. Coming down from one of those double rollers, Berton flew past us about three feet in the air; he slammed into the rear bolster cushion and then lay there for a few seconds as we pounded on, ever on.

That night at the hotel bar at Morro Bay, Betty Cook pulled a twenty dollar bill out of her purse. It was dripping wet.

The next morning at the seven o'clock drivers' meeting, Nordskog gave us the good news. "Santa Barbara is completely socked in," he announced. In addition, fifty miles down the coast at Point Conception the wind was up to 25 knots and the seas were running at twelve feet. Nordskog postponed the start for an hour and then, in the interest of safety, asked all the drivers to run together in a pack until we rounded Point Conception. Koster on our Cigarette was to be the leader, in the middle, with the other boats spread out on our left and right. The idea was always to keep the boat next to you in sight. "It can get awful lonesome out there if you're lost in the fog," Nordskog said. Then, reassuringly, he urged us to clear the point by at least three miles, saying, "There are submerged rocks out there as big as this room." Koster took some more Rolaids.

When we got down to the dock it was so foggy that we couldn't see the second line of moored sailboats. The harbormaster had to lead us out of the bay for the start. But oddly enough, given the individualistic instincts of most speedboat drivers, the pack idea actually worked. Racing through the fog, Reggie Fountain stayed just off our starboard quarter; the Cobalt was just beyond him. About twenty yards off our port quarter, Dick Genth kept formation in his Chris-Craft; Sandy Satullo, driving a Wellcraft Scarab 38, came in and out of the fog just beyond him.

After an hour or so we cleared the point, and a few

minutes later the fog blew away, revealing patches of blue sky. Just as we felt the sunshine we heard the roar of a low-flying plane and Koster's twin-engine Cessna, searching for us, passed overhead. We all cheered and waved; it saw us, went into a slow turn and then flew by again, fifty yards off the deck, wagging its wings. We cheered some more. It felt very good that somebody knew where we were. The plane stayed with us all the way into Santa Barbara.

Then we hit the shark. In the clearing fog we all saw it at the same time, about ten yards in front of the boat, the dorsal fin out of the water, the shape of the body unmistakable. There was no time to turn; we hit it broadside, the propellers making only a slight *chunk* as they churned over the hide. Barely losing a beat, the Cigarette sped on. We turned around and saw a pool of blood starting to spread in the water.

By the time we got to Santa Barbara, only three of the original seven boats were still in the race. Genth with his fast Chris-Craft was in first place; we were thirty-seven minutes behind in our Cigarette, and Reggie Fountain was fifteen minutes behind us in his Fountain Executioner.

Our strategy up to now had been to take it fairly easy, to keep the engines at 4800 to 4900 rpm and to let the powerful Cigarette, probably the strongest offshore hull on the market, keep us running through the rough water while the other boats developed problems. Now, going into the final stretch from Santa Barbara to Long Beach, we knew that Genth's smaller boat was faster than we were; unless he broke down we couldn't catch him. Our problem was to stay in second place, to keep Reggie Fountain in his swift, light Executioner from making up too much time in the flat water ahead of us.

The weather was no problem anymore; we left Santa Barbara after noon in the clear, and along with Genth and Fountain, we simply flew down the coast. For the last leg, Jerry Berton took the wheel, inching the throttles ahead as we got closer to the finish.

Before the race, Nordskog had said the buoy marking the entrance to the Long Beach harbor would be visible for miles. A weather balloon would be flying above it; a thirty-eight-foot committee boat would be next to it. This Sunday afternoon, however, we saw the buoy clearly enough—but no balloon, no committee boat. So we cut inside the buoy, by now racing flat out, screaming over the surface, speeding inside the harbor, thinking only of the finish—cheering as we flew past the stern of the Queen Mary.

Exhausted, still excited, we tied up the Cigarette and were climbing up on the dock, when suddenly Gloria Sanders, Kees' wife, came running toward us waving a VHF handheld radio. "The committee says you missed the buoy," she shouted. "You have to go back."

Kees grabbed the keys and fired up the engines as the rest of us simply tumbled into the boat, pulling in lines after us. One more time, flying low, determined after all this not to lose by a technicality. Full throttle out of the harbor, roaring around the buoy, screaming again into the harbor, past the Sunday crowds, past the Queen Mary.

Unbelievably, just as we had the boat tied up again, Gloria Sanders came running back down the dock waving the handheld. "They said you didn't have your helmets and jackets on," she called. "You have to put them on and do it again." We all did a double-take to see if she was kidding. She wasn't. Once again Kees started the engines; once again we fell into the boat, catching lines as we went. This time, however, we all rummaged around the cockpit where we had thrown our racing helmets and our life jackets, each putting on the nearest one.

Once again around the buoy and back to the harbor, except that by this time we were all too frustrated to cheer as we crossed the line. I couldn't help thinking, as we tied up again, that this was the only race I had ever finished three times.

After we found the committee room, we learned that we had come in second. The running times, from San Francisco to Long Beach: Chris-Craft, 9:03; Cigarette, 9:53; Fountain: 9:55. That night, at the awards banquet on the Queen Mary, Nordskog declared a tie for second place, allowing that in a 423-mile race, a two-minute difference was not significant.

Two nights later, finally back in my own bed, I woke in the middle of the night with a start. My pajamas were wet with sweat. I had been dreaming—of the fog.

August, 1984

⚓

AMERICAN HERO

Dodge Morgan, a fifty-four-year-old Maine newspaper pub-
lisher, sails alone around the world in a record 150 days—
without stopping.

BY POLLY WHITTELL

For Dodge Morgan, the tensest moment of his
record-breaking nonstop solo circumnavigation of the
world came while he was swaying aloft up his seventy-
five-foot-high mast in the middle of the South Atlantic
Ocean, trying to fix some broken rigging. Suddenly a
squall came through, throwing his sixty-foot cutter *Ameri-*
can Promise into a violent accidental jibe. As the boom
slammed from one side of the boat to the other, the
whisker pole extending the headsail snapped its preventer
line and smashed into Morgan's shoulder, almost knocking him off the mast, and bruising him badly. Despite the
intense pain, he managed to hang on, showing the grit
and determination that got him through many tough
times during his 150 days, one hour, and six minutes at
sea, covering 27,600 miles.

Morgan was not just out to set a record. The fifty-four-year-old newspaper publisher from Cape Elizabeth, Maine, hoped to be the first American to sail around the world alone without stopping—and to break the existing record of 292 days set by Englishman Chay Blyth in 1971. But his greater purpose was "to challenge my own soul, spirit, and the will of self-preservation to their limits, never giving up—it's pushing yourself to the edge. Sailing a small boat alone is such an uncomplicated way. I'll be entering that psychological fourth dimension . . . but that intrigues me," he said at the start.

The voyage was the fulfillment of a dream Morgan had had since the age of thirty, when he spent two years sailing his thirty-six-foot wooden schooner *Coaster* from Maine to Alaska via the Panama Canal and several Pacific islands. It was in Alaska that he promised himself he'd sail around the world alone someday.

After working as a reporter for the *Anchorage Daily News* (he has a degree in journalism from Boston University), and then heading up an advertising/public relations firm, Morgan returned to his native Massachusetts. There, with a $25,000 investment and his garage as his office, he founded Controlonics Corp., an electronics firm that he later sold for $32 million, giving him the time and resources to fulfill his plan. He relocated to Maine; where he also acquired *The Maine Times*.

Morgan felt he had the requisite physical and mental stamina for the voyage. Besides being in good shape, he said, "I have a strong will and a singular determination to succeed; I do not easily give up. What I learned about myself from those years aboard *Coaster* formed a very important part of my self-knowledge. But I'm not sure *now* how well I know myself, and it's time to try again to find out."

For this trip, Morgan wanted a heavy-displacement vessel with a very seakindly hull—"a no-compromise boat." The $1.5 million sixty-footer was designed by former America's Cup skipper Ted Hood and built by Hood's Little Harbor boatyard. "While no boat is free from danger," Morgan said, "if there was ever a boat designed to reduce the risks, it's this one."

He wanted *American Promise* to be fast, but also designed to minimize skipper fatigue. He said he'd gladly give up half a knot of speed for a hull that would allow him to get a good night's sleep. The boat was given a waterline length of fifty-six feet, a 59,500-pound displacement, and a generous 17'2" beam. She had a massive rudder, a centerline daggerboard that could also act as an emergency rudder, and two diagonal daggerboards that could be lowered independently. Contributing to her stability were 18,000 pounds of ballast down in her 10-foot-draft fin keel. Her sturdy, high-tech composite construction of fiberglass incorporating bulletproof Kevlar and Airex was designed to help her withstand sustained high winds and knockdowns. With five watertight compartments and submarine-type doors, she was even built to handle a 360-degree rollover.

To make her a singlehanded vessel, *American Promise* had a Hood Sto-way mainsail and Sea Furl roller-reefing headsails that could be extended outward on whisker poles. Thirteen electric winches controlled the halyards and lines for the boat's 1,614 square feet of sail with the push of a button (though there were manual overrides for everything).

Redundancy was built in throughout the boat. There were three sets of sails, as well as several electrical power sources, including four banks of batteries, a 160-horsepower Perkins diesel engine that could be used for re-charging them, and an array of solar panels. The boat also had a vast suite of electronics, including an Epson computer linked to Datamarine instrumentation, two satellite navigation units, two lorans, a weather fax, a radar, a depthfinder, and various radios.

For emergencies, Morgan had an Avon life raft, a sur-vival suit, EPIRB emergency beacons, a medical kit, and 650 pounds of tools and spare parts. An Argos transponder allowed home base to track the boat's progress via satellite.

For sustenance, his wife, Manny, provided 1,600 pounds of food (even sweet-and-sour shrimp) and pow-dered drinks, based on advice from a nutritionist. Most of it was freeze-dried, vacuum-packed or canned, and di-vided into menus that rotated every twenty-one days. Morgan also carried 275 pounds of clothing, most of it foul-weather gear, and 200 pairs of socks (courtesy of his mother-in-law), so that he'd have a clean pair each day. Stuffed in the toes of the socks were sayings and jokes on scraps of paper.

What he'd miss most, Morgan said, was his family—Manny and the children, Hoyt, eleven, and Kimberly, eight. Although at first she'd been less than enthusiastic about the trip, as the departure date drew closer, Manny became "very excited, because Dodge has been planning this for so long," she said.

But two weeks before Morgan's planned departure from Portland, Maine, Hurricane Gloria dashed his brand-new yacht—and almost his hopes—against the rocks near his home. Fortunately, it turned out that only the rudder had sustained serious damage and it was quickly repaired.

Back on track again, Morgan appeared at Portland's DiMillo's Marina on Columbus Day decked out in a tuxedo for his sendoff. Asked what would help him the most, he joked, "the wind behind my back"—at which point the air became absolutely still. *American Promise* had to be towed to the Portland Head Light by a lobsterboat.

Then, not long into the voyage, two gales hit back to back, packing 50-knot winds and twenty-foot seas. A headsail halyard parted, forcing Morgan to climb the mast of the violently rolling boat to fix it. All the while a whale almost as big as the boat lay on its back watching the spectacle from alongside.

No sooner was the headsail problem solved than the autopilot system—not heavy-duty enough to handle the beefy boat in big seas—stopped functioning. Morgan exhausted himself hand-steering the boat with neither sleep nor food for four days and nights straight. Finally, he was forced to change course and put in at Bermuda for repairs.

"Morgan seemed crushed and beaten by the setback at first," said Bob Rice of Weather Services Corp., who gave Morgan twice-weekly forecasts by radio. "But he bounded right back."

This time the starting point for the voyage would be Bermuda. But this time, Morgan was worried. He had lost almost three weeks and would have to race the clock to get around South America's treacherous Cape Horn before the unforgiving Southern Ocean winter, with its added danger of icebergs, set in.

A week out of Bermuda, Morgan lost another day veering out of the path of Hurricane Kate, and was still getting hit by 45-knot winds and twenty-five-foot seas. But *American Promise* was moving southward faster than her skipper or designer had dreamed possible. (She would average 7.1 knots and 171.9 miles a day over the course of the voyage.) When he crossed the Equator a week ahead of

schedule, Morgan celebrated by flushing the toilet repeatedly to watch the water swirl counterclockwise rather
than clockwise, as it does in the Northern Hemisphere.
And despite the scary accidental jibe that occurred on this
stretch, he breezed on to South Africa's Cape of Good
Hope in time for a rounding on Christmas day.

"That's when I knew I could do it in 180 days or better," he said. He had already made up more than half the
time lost in Bermuda. He celebrated by making a long
radio call to his family, opening gifts they had sent along
(smoked salmon, a rum cake, a poem, and a tube of Su-
perglue), and singing Christmas carols.

But in the Indian Ocean the weather turned horrendous, delivering at least three major-league storms with
winds of 50 to 60 knots. In the worst of these, Morgan
saw forty-five-foot waves so steep that *American Promise*
would periodically come over a crest, then fall through
the air and crash on her beam at the bottom of the trough.
There was one knockdown that flung him headlong into
a door handle and gave him a black eye, and another that
jolted the engine's V-drive off its mounts. This meant the
diesel would be useless in the event of an emergency for
the rest of the voyage.

But Morgan was still making good time—indeed, he occasionally surfed down the waves at 23 knots. On January
15—his birthday—he logged 236 miles, the best day of
the voyage. And by Super Bowl Sunday, he'd reached the
halfway point, just south of Tasmania.

About two weeks into the Pacific, as he entered the
"Screaming 50s" latitudes, Morgan encountered the worst
storm of the voyage, Tropical Cyclone Ima. Winds gusting
to 75 knots and forty-five- to fifty-foot waves battered
American Promise for three days. It was weather that was

rough enough, he said, "to jerk the jam off a cracker. It would stop your heart and take your breath away to sit there and look up at these seas coming at you," Morgan said. "They were just enormous, mountainous, with the tops curling and breaking over the transom, filling the cockpit with water. I was floating around, hanging on, trying to retrieve lines that kept washing overboard. Horizontal rain and sleet were stinging like the devil. Sometimes I'd just say okay, that's enough for now, let up— but it wouldn't. It made me start to think maybe it wasn't going to. That was the difficult part."

He got through such situations a minute at a time. "I'd think *I may not be able to get through this storm, but I can get through the next minute.* Each time you reach the edge, somehow you push it so the next time it doesn't seem as bad." Yet, he said, he was not afraid of dying. "Death is something you come to grips with beforehand."

Ima dealt Morgan several knockdowns. "After the first two or three," he said, "it didn't seem to make much difference. It was very inconvenient—you had to pick everything up. But the boat didn't seem to mind."

When Morgan radioed home to report on the storm, it was the only time Manny ever heard him say the words, "*if* I make it." Ima had so exhausted him that when warned that a 400-foot-long iceberg was drifting into his path, all he could do was joke, "I'll tell the first mate to keep a lookout." (Fortunately, he never encountered it.) In a later conversation he quipped to Rice, "I think I've taken this going south for the winter much, much too far."

After a long series of squalls and one more big storm, Morgan was treated to good weather when he finally reached Cape Horn—his first sighting of land since leaving

Bermuda. It was February 28, his wedding anniversary. Legend has it that Cape Horn doesn't let sailors by unless they've earned it. The Horn let Morgan by easy. He was able to pass within a mile and a half, with excellent visibility. He described the Cape as "awesome; it looks almost like a lion's head, with the tooth—a sheer cliff—coming down to the sea and the mane rising back north." Donning his tuxedo, Morgan opened three splits of champagne. "I gave a huge war whoop and threw one toward the Horn, poured the second over the boat, and poured the third into me."

While there were no big storms on the homeward stretch back to Bermuda, Morgan spent one of his most difficult weeks beating against stiff northwesterlies off Rio that caused him to sprain his back while working on deck. But the very worst day of the voyage, he says, came as he was going through the doldrums at the Equator. "All around me the ocean was a clear, glassy mirror. It was hot, hazy, humid, horrible. I'd see a puff of wind and go over toward the ripple and find out it was shark fins. I was surrounded by sharks."

Yet Morgan was amazed at how few living things he saw during 80 percent of the voyage. He spotted only two vessels—one sailboat in the Atlantic on the way out, and one ship with an Arabic name in the Indian Ocean—before reaching the shipping lanes near Bermuda. And aside from a handful of flying fish, sharks, porpoises, whales, and albatross, "I often saw no birds or fish, no life at all. That's when you really feel alone." It was particularly desolate in the Southern Ocean, which he describes as a "lousy place, not fit for man or beast." After one long stretch of nothing but air and sea, he told Rice he sometimes wondered if the whole voyage were "a hoax and

I'm nowhere near where I think I am. I've had no visual confirmation of anything." He now says the experience has given him a deeper respect for living creatures and the conviction that man should not interfere with the world's natural order.

Although Morgan had found breaking away from his family and civilization "very, very painful," he got used to the solitude after about the first three weeks. His radios provided his "social life" through a network of ham operators. He also admitted, "I talked to myself a lot, though I never screamed or shouted." He would sometimes carry on dialogues in two voices—a deep, sophisticated voice of reason passing judgment and a less rational falsetto voice.

Once he accidentally added a quart of orange juice instead of milk to some clam chowder, and called out, "Hey, everybody come see what this idiot has done now—let's force him to eat it." His sense of humor kept him going. "The worse things got, the more I tried to find something funny. You have to laugh when there's nothing else you can do," he said.

Among his greatest sources of amusement were his daily "shrink tests." Before leaving, he'd signed on as a guinea pig for two Boston University psychologists studying the effects of long-term isolation. "Can you imagine anything more ridiculous than being in the middle of the ocean, rolling around in forty-five-foot waves, and the assignment is to answer questions like: 'Do you think you're attractive?' 'Do you feel you are the life of the party?' *Hell, I am the only party here!*"

When Morgan wasn't working at keeping the boat moving, there were plenty of other things to keep him busy. His daily routine began at 5:30 AM with a tour of the boat, trimming sails, having coffee, and shaving. After brunch he'd take his position and make his noon log entry (he wrote 60,000 words in all). Afternoons were spent on chores and preventive maintenance, taking naps and making radio contacts. At sunset he did his "shrink tests," ate supper, and retired. He managed eight hours of sleep a day in two-hour segments, getting up to check the rigging periodically. But he says he got no real rest, because of the constant apprehension: "You have to be on your guard even when you're asleep." His weekly showers provided the only time he felt really good—"pure ecstasy," he said.

Morgan only used about half the provisions he had on board. The only things he ran out of were dry cereal, Jiffy popcorn and beer (a friend had left a case on board). He joked that his most frightening moment was "picking the next to last bottle of beer out of the bilge." In general, he said, "the food was lousy—I have fired the cook."

Cannon fire, parades, bands playing the "Star Spangled Banner," hundreds of flag-wavers, and a crowd of reporters hailed the end of Morgan's voyage at St. George's Harbour, Bermuda. Morgan had cut the previous record nearly in half. At that point only nine men on record had ever completed such a voyage, and he was indeed the first American. (The rules, per *The Guinness Book of World Records*, bar setting foot ashore, receiving help or assistance, or having any direct contact with any person.)

The biggest surprise for the family, friends and spectators aboard the flotilla boats that went out to greet *American Promise* at the finish was that both the boat and her skipper looked as though they were just returning from a Sunday sail. With barely a smudge or a scratch on her, *American Promise* came bounding gracefully toward the line in a brisk 20-knot breeze, making better than 9 knots of speed, and as she crossed it, a beaming Morgan triumphantly fired a red flare.

When told over the radio that the boat looked good, Morgan quipped, "Well she's only been used once." Turning to the onlookers lining the deck of the tugboat *Bermudian*, he exclaimed, "You all look so beautiful. I haven't seen anybody for so long, and now there's a whole bunch of people. I can't tell you how beautiful you all look."

When Morgan reached the dock and set foot on terra firma for the first time in five months, he leapt in the air with a loud "Whoopee." Then he was granted his first three wishes: hugs from Manny and the children; a cheeseburger on a silver platter, and a vodka-tonic. "This is quite a spectacle," he said to the crowd. "I'm glad I got here in time to see it all."

Looking back on the voyage, Morgan says it allowed him to sort out and firm up his priorities. He gained "a renewed understanding that what makes life worth living is other people . . . the variety, the excitement, the chaos and the screwups that are so wonderful.

"As beautiful as solitude can be, as close to the truth as you can come in the presence of the sea, and as satisfying as the long string of little victories that add up to a voyage like this, I have decided that the race I want to belong to is the human race—and to hell with that stuff out there."

July, 1986

⚓

SHIPWRECKED

A transatlantic record attempt ends in disaster—after which, the crippled sailboat is nearly crushed by the ship that comes to its rescue.

BY DAG PIKE

I have been across the Atlantic in many types of craft from high-tech record-breakers to staid old cargo ships. On one of my first crossings, in a freighter, we spent thirty-six hours in a life-or-death situation during a bad storm. Every time the ship rolled, with its shifting cargo, we thought it would be the last. I should have learned my lesson, but forty years later, in 1985, during an attempt with Richard Branson to break the transatlantic powerboat record, I was shipwrecked when the sixty-five-foot *Virgin Atlantic Challenger* broke up and sank 138 miles from the finish.

Nevertheless, this spring I was out there again, trying to break the transatlantic sailing record. Having finally set the powerboat record three years ago in the new seventy-two-foot *Virgin Atlantic,* here was a chance for a great double—to hold both the power and sailing records.

But this time the Atlantic won. We needed strong winds to give the seventy-five-foot sailing catamaran *Chaffoteaux Challenger* the speed to cross the ocean in seven days. The Atlantic responded with the strong winds we wanted, but they came from all points of the compass, generating wild, confused seas in an awesome display of nature's strength that left us weak and gasping and crying for help. Every time we thought it couldn't get any worse, it always did.

Chaffoteaux Challenger was built for speed, with very little compromise in the way of luxury and comfort. One of the largest sailing catamarans afloat, she was nearly the size of a tennis court, with a towering 100-foot mast on which to hang the sails that powered her to speeds of up to 25 knots.

Accommodations were very basic—a sleeping cabin in each side hull, and the navigation and galley areas in the main crossbeam that connected the two hulls, on which the mast was stepped. There were open steering cockpits on each side, where the helmsman controlled this flying monster, wide open to the elements and often up to his neck in water.

We knew it was going to be a rough, tough ride. To set a new record we had to average 17 knots, which called for strong winds all the way. The highly experienced seven-man crew from the United Kingdom (with Peter Phillips as skipper and me as navigator) assembled in New York City when the forecasts predicted a strong westerly airflow over the Atlantic, and it was with hope in our hearts that we crossed the Ambrose Light starting line.

The first couple of days were going to be critical. Here we had to negotiate with the flow of lows up the East Coast to find favorable winds to take us out into the main westerly flow. We set off into a full northerly gale in the hope that this would rapidly switch to the west and give us the early boost we needed.

Instead, we were forced south all night, but the wind relented as we picked up the favorable Gulf Stream. Now we were on our way in earnest, we thought, but the wind fizzled away to nothing and left us floundering.

Dampness had permeated the electronic instruments, so we couldn't pick up the weather chaps, but this was no time to give up. And soon we were rewarded with freshening winds from the west. So far, so good.

The speed and our hopes rose, and all day we bowled along under a strong wind. We could make up lost time and still be on schedule for the record. But the Atlantic would not let us get away so lightly. If we had known what was in store, we would have been hightailing it back to New York. The Atlantic was playing games with us, egging us along into deeper and deeper trouble.

The warning signs were out the next day, with a northeasterly gale and a wild, confused sea. Hours later, the wind was back in the southwest and there was an equally wild display of thunder and lightning. Everyone on board was wet, and one of the biggest luxuries going on watch was to put on *damp* socks rather than *wet* ones. But the galley was still producing hot soups and food, and we were in no mood to give in just because of a little discomfort. We were now almost halfway across.

The contest began heating up that night when the wind went berserk. All hands were on deck shortening sail when a violent squall struck. You could hear the shriek of the wind as the squall approached, then hit us with winds of close to 100 knots. The only thing to do was head off downwind and pray as everything went flying.

Heading off the top of one wave at 25 knots, we left

the water completely, and skipped the top of the next wave before landing with a sickening crunch: Both hulls were cracked. Almost continuous lightning illuminated the scene while thunder provided the sound effects. Having doubtless set a new record as the world's largest wind-surfer with our flying leap, at this point we abandoned hope for the sailing record from New York to England—survival was now the name of the game.

After the squall, the wind began running around the clock, first westerly, then northerly, then southwesterly, all the time close to gale-force. With just a scrap of jib showing, we eased the boat in the huge, confused seas, which towered thirty feet above us. When daylight brought welcome relief, it was short-lived, as we saw the extent of the damage. The hull cracks ran down each side of both cockpits, spelling deep trouble.

I wanted us to get to the southeast to try to clear this violent weather but we were forced to go with the wind, attempting to reduce the stress on the damaged hulls. The log shows the wind from all directions for the next couple of days, rarely below Force 7, with the crew getting weaker and weaker as the near constant bucket bailing took its toll. Sleeping on air beds acted as a bilge alarm. When the bed started floating you knew it was time to start bailing.

After a week at sea and 1,000 hard-won miles behind us—when we thought things could not possibly get worse—the Atlantic still had more in store. We were now trying to nurse the boat along to the Azores, almost 1,000 miles ahead, for repairs, but the wind kept growing.

Running before a strong gale from the west with towering twenty-five-foot seas coming up astern, *Chaffoteaux Challenger* was suddenly picked up by a gust of wind and accelerated out of control, flying down the face of a wave at about 30 knots. As I stood by the mast, I saw this near-vertical wall of water ahead—the back of the next wave—and was suddenly half underwater as the bows buried themselves in it. Then slowly, the water cleared and the bows rose. How we didn't pitchpole I will never know, but our port rudder was ripped away.

Now we were losing the battle in a big way, and while we were down, the Atlantic hit us with yet another, even more ferocious storm, from the northwest. As Force 10 winds pushed up thirty- to forty-foot seas, we had to stream warps to try to keep the boat stable and ease the pressure on the steering. Even under bare poles we were still running at about 10 knots, which wasn't helping the hull cracks. When daylight came we could see them getting bigger, opening over an inch at their tops and extending nearly halfway around the hulls.

The Azores were still over 800 miles away and the chance of making port safely was diminishing. We were about as far from any point of land as it's possible to be on the Atlantic. During the night, as the cracks continued to grow, water rushed in and bailing became an all-too-regular burden on each watch. Haggard faces, red-rimmed eyes, and saltwater sores told the story of the exhausted men. Both crew and boat were getting weaker by the minute and we now knew it was time to get out before the Atlantic dealt its death blow. We decided to call for help.

We contacted the Coast Guard in the morning, and with great efficiency they located a ship about three hours away and steered it toward us. Within an hour, the 950-foot *Sealand Performance*, one of the world's largest container ships, was in direct radio contact. All we could do now was prepare for evacuation and wait. The waiting was the worst part—it gives you time to think of all the things that might go wrong in a rescue. And although the wind had dropped to Force 6, there was still a heavy swell running, so we knew the rescue was not going to be easy.

Parking a mammoth ship alongside our boat would be difficult even in the best of conditions, and we were full of apprehension as the towering sides of the *Sealand Performance* loomed astern. The captain did a superb job of alignment, but with the speed and movement of the ship in the swells and with its deck forty feet above us, we were unable to get lines made fast and we drifted astern. The real trouble started when our rigging caught in a door frame in the ship's side, stopping our boat dead in the water. The catamaran's mast couldn't stand the strain and suddenly, three-quarters of a ton of mast and rigging came crashing down on deck.

As we all scrambled to get away from the tumbling mast and wires, I dove for cover inside the crossbeam, which seemed like a good idea at the time. But then, devoid of her mast, the *Chaffoteaux Challenger* suddenly got washed under the stern of the ship near its propellers. I remember looking out quickly and seeing the ship's stern lift in the swell and our boat being sucked in underneath. Once more I dove for cover as the huge stern came crashing down on top of us. The noise was horrendous and I watched in horror as the space I was in was squashed, the fragile fairing crushed under the pressure. It all seemed to happen in slow motion. I really thought it was the end when, with just two feet of headroom left, water started pouring in as our boat was forced under the surface.

But then, all of a sudden I could see daylight again. The boat had popped up clear and I leapt out of my hole as though rocket-propelled. Miraculously, the rest of the crew was all there, too. They had all found some refuge on deck and, though drenched and shaken, everyone had survived without injury.

With our boat even more badly damaged by this drama, we now drifted helplessly. It took a seemingly eternal twenty minutes for the *Sealand Performance* to come around for another attempt. To restore some sort of normalcy to our shattered nerves as we waited, we sat there eating some peaches, trying to pretend that having a 60,000-ton ship sit on you was an everyday occurrence.

But the second time around, the ship's crew had everything ready and did a splendid job. Once safely alongside, it took them only a matter of minutes to get us up the ship's side on the pilot hoist, a sort of mechanical rope ladder. It felt wonderful to have solid steel decks under our feet.

But as we headed back the way we'd come, even the huge container ship had a rough ride in the stormy seas. One other small disaster: This being a United States ship meant no alcohol on board, and we would have all welcomed a drink. The night of the rescue I couldn't sleep— I kept trembling like a leaf. But the hospitality on board was excellent, and five days later we arrived safely in Charleston, South Carolina.

In the early stages of the crossing, we had gotten badly out of step with the weather patterns we'd planned on because we weren't able to make enough speed. The Atlantic showed no mercy, and I think we were lucky to escape with our lives. My respect for this mightiest of oceans has grown. To escape three times is about the measure of luck anyone can expect, and I don't feel like making a go at the transatlantic sailing record again any time soon. On the other hand, if I had a dollar for every time I've said such a thing, I'd be a rich man.

July, 1989

⚓

VENEZUELAN JUSTICE

During a South American cruise on a sixty-one-foot Feadship, two Americans are suddenly arrested and sentenced to rot in jail.

BY JOHN W. SMITH, AS TOLD TO ROY ATTAWAY

It is a little after 4:00 AM when the bell begins to ring. I hear the guards coming down the corridor, running keys along the steel bars like kids passing a picket fence. They are shouting in Spanish. *"Numeros! Numeros!"*

The cacophony is underscored by the muttered replies and imprecations of the inmates, like some obscene *obbligato*. Across from me, the Egyptian rolls over and curses. He is a pleasant enough man—if you overlook the fact that he tried to butcher some companions with a machete.

The wave of noise reaches our cell and lights snap on. The light is hard and bright and the glare off the dingy yellow walls is painful. The fat man in the corner, an accused embezzler, breaks wind loudly. I doubt that it will be noticed among the rancid odors of last night's cooking.

Harvey swings his legs over the edge of his bunk and gives me a baleful look. He starts to say something but changes his mind and we shuffle across the floor with the rest of the men. We are all tired and bored. It is one of those mornings when words seem futile—superfluous even. Everything seems futile. Harvey and I know what each other is thinking. Not so much *how the hell did we get into this mess,* but *how and when are we going to get out of this mess?* How, indeed, could a leisurely cruise through the Caribbean end up in a Venezuelan prison cell?

There is a cautionary lesson here for all yachtsmen.

One by one we shout off our numbers and are readmitted to the ennui of cell life. There are nineteen of us this week in a cell with sixteen bunks. I pity the poor bastards who sleep on the floor. I know how they feel: I spent the first two weeks sleeping there myself. There are no rats, thank God, but cockroaches skitter silently down the grease-filmed walls in the darkness.

After the head count is taken the hubbub subsides and the lights are turned off again. We lie back down on our bunks and try to recapture the sweet release of sleep. A dog barks in a nearby alley and in the distance a truck sings down a highway. I manage to doze, but the familiar spectres of anxiety insinuate themselves into my thoughts. It is a nightmare that has lasted for two and a half months.

Shortly after 7:30 on the morning of October 12, Harvey and I eased *Sea Wind,* a sixty-one-foot Feadship, up to the fuel dock at Caraballeda Yacht Club in Macuto, a coastal suburb of Caracas. We were tired from the overnight run from Curaçao, but happy in the extreme. We had taken five and a half weeks to cruise down from Tampa-St. Petersburg, Florida, a pleasant odyssey through the Bahamas with Harvey's wife and daughter, some other friends, and a maid. The others had either gone ahead to Caracas, where Harvey (an American businessman) and his wife have an apartment, or flown back to the States, leaving the two of us to make the final 150-mile leg.

We were told by the dockmaster that there were no customs or immigration facilities in Macuto and that we would have to go to Guaira, the main commercial port. We filled *Sea Wind*'s nearly empty tanks (at nine cents a gallon for diesel we were beginning to feel really good about Venezuela) and backtracked along the coast. We radioed ahead and were met by three customs agents on a pilot boat. In the middle of taking our declaration, they suddenly announced that we would have to return the next day because it was a national holiday (Columbus Day) and they were no longer on duty. Harvey and I shrugged at the minor inconvenience and returned to Macuto where we were met by Harvey's wife and the maid, who was to clean up the boat. We had wasted a day, but still were euphoric at having finished the long journey. Accordingly, we went into town to celebrate. We did not know, could not have known, that already we were being fed into the blind maw of the Venezuelan bureaucracy.

The maid called around 8:30 that evening. There were soldiers on the boat, she said. They had been there earlier in the afternoon and had returned. We'd better come.

We were apprehensive when we saw the boat literally ringed by armed men, but not yet alarmed. We had done nothing wrong. Venezuela is a good neighbor. Surely these were reasonable men. It was not until they began to question us about a .357 magnum revolver and an AR-15 rifle that an unease settled in my stomach. Harvey calmly acknowledged ownership of the weapons, explained that they were carried for personal protection (pirates are a very real danger along the north coast of South

America), that they had been declared in other countries with no problems, and that we had tried to declare them that morning in Guaira. None of this made any impression on the officer in charge of the detail. We laughed at his implication that we were gun runners. We did not laugh very long.

We were taken to the Guardia Nacional headquarters and questioned until 2 AM the following morning and then taken back to the boat for another search. (Later we discovered that in addition to the guns, the soldiers had also looted a 35mm camera and some silver jewelry). The maid, meanwhile, had locked the boat and we had no key, so we were taken back to guard headquarters. My apprehension was deepened by the fact that most of the conversation was in Spanish, which Harvey speaks but I do not.

"They want a bribe," Harvey said at one point. It was about 3:30 AM.

"How much?"

"About a thousand American," he said. "I've already explained that we don't have that much cash but could get it."

Apparently it was not enough. The guard officers were becoming increasingly nervous and finally, at around 7:30 on the morning of the thirteenth, we were told we were going to be charged with possession of contraband and suspicion of smuggling. Absurd but no longer laughable.

The chronology that follows is incredible in the most horrific sense of the word.

First we were driven in a prison van to Caracas where a search warrant was sought for house and boat (why bother, we wondered). The house was searched and the boat was moved to the Guardia Nacional dock in Guaira where another search was carried out. It was then we discovered the missing camera and jewelry. All the while, the Guardia officers ignored our pleas to check with the nearby customs agents.

For the next three days, we were held on the boat under guard. Held incommunicado, so the soldiers thought. Unbeknownst to them, we were in constant touch with Harvey's wife and the U.S. Coast Guard in New Orleans via the boat's single sideband radio. Nothing, no one, seemed able to help.

On Monday we made a statement at Guardia headquarters and then were asked to sign a Spanish language copy. Unable to translate it properly, we refused. We again were denied permission to contact customs.

On Wednesday, our spirits were momentarily lifted when our lawyer (retained by Harvey's wife) managed to get a writ of habeus corpus. But the press also got wind of the story and we were splashed across the pages of local papers as infamous smugglers. The judge promptly cancelled the writ and on Friday we were taken to the Municipal Prison at Catia in downtown Caracas.

Our first weekend in prison was marked by the violent onset of dysentery from eating prison food. (I lost thirty-five pounds in all while there. It was not until we understood the system of bribing guards that Harvey's wife was able to bring us food and clean clothing.)

On October 24, twelve days after our arrival, we were ushered into the chambers of Dr. Luis Ramirez Grazziani, a judge. Now begins the really incredible part: We spend the entire day in the judge's office making and signing statements and answering questions. The *Fiscal del Ministerio Publics*, or public prosecutor, stated that he thought the state had no case and recommended our release. The judge, evidently upset at having been detained until 5:30 (we were told he usually works only until 3:30) decided to "teach (us) a lesson." We were declared guilty and remanded to prison.

Case closed. Just like that.

For the next two months we sat in prison while friends on the outside tried to pry us from the grip of the Venezuelan judiciary. Involved in this fight were not only our families and Venezuelan friends of Harvey's, but the United States Consul General and, eventually, Ambassador to the United Nations Andrew Young, and Speaker of the U.S. House of Representatives Thomas P. "Tip" O'Neill! Most of the leverage for this high-level intervention came as the result of some dogged work by Rep. C. W. "Bill" Young (R-Fla.), our local congressman.

Still the antiquated machinery of Venezuelan law would not budge. We were sent word through our new attorney, a highly esteemed criminal lawyer, that a judge of the Superior Court would set us free in a matter of hours if we would compensate him for his time. To the tune of $40,000. We sent word back to tell him what he could do with it. Where the sun never shines, as they say. Maybe it was just Yankee stubbornness but somewhere the tattered faith in justice and fair play prevailed. We were determined to fight it through the courts.

It is a terrifying experience to know that your fate is in someone else's hands and that you not only are powerless to do anything yourself, you aren't even really sure what is happening on the outside. Our only source of information was notes smuggled in with our food every day.

What was happening was that all of the pressure brought to bear was finally setting the legal machinery in motion. The grease that kept it from shuddering to a stop again was a bribe of 200 Bolivares (about $48) to the chief secretary in Judge Grazziani's office to keep our file on top of the pile, and a "present" of an $1,800 gold watch to the *Fiscal*.

God only knows what happens to people with no money and no friends.

To give you an idea of the "justice" meted out under this system, one of our fellow inmates was an aircraft mechanic. He had worked on a Venezuelan airliner that subsequently crashed with loss of life. Even though no cause was determined, the mechanic was held in prison for more than two years. You definitely are guilty until proven innocent.

It is now December 22. For the past week, Harvey and I have been living in comparative luxury in a cell designed for three. It is locked only at night. But freedom is relative. We are still in prison. Today is supposed to be the day of our release. We have coffee and talk about it cautiously. It is supposed to happen. But it was supposed to have happened so many times before that we have come to view such news with a mixture of hope and cynicism.

Throughout the day we wait. By noon I am convinced that there has been yet another foulup. Miraculously, at 2:30, Harvey's wife, U.S. Consul General Howard Gross, and a friend arrive, smiling. There are whoops and tears of joy.

True to form, it takes an hour and a half to sign the requisite papers and finally we head for the prison entrance. The guard there orders us to stop. Who are we? Where are we going? He is rude to the point of surliness. We show him our papers. He directs his attention to me and asks in Spanish what I was in prison for. And two and a half months of frustration and bitterness finally erupt.

"Nada," I spat back at him. *"Nada a todo."* Nothing. Nothing at all.

The following morning, I am on a Pan Am flight to Miami. Behind and below, the Caribbean sparkles its old siren of sun and sea and the round, brown mountains of Venezuela fade into the blue haze. It will take considerably longer for the nightmare to die.

March, 1979

⚓

HEROES

At midnight, 200 miles offshore, in 60-knot winds and twenty-five-foot seas, the Coast Guard saves three shipwrecked sailors.

BY JOANNE A. FISHMAN

As the 256-foot container ship *Lloyd Bermuda* powered into the cold, dark North Atlantic Ocean on a midwinter Tuesday from New York Harbor, a massive cold front swept eastward. The frontal system burst across the New York area the next day, with 60 mile-per-hour winds and severe thunderstorms.

The front continued eastward, seas built up to twenty-five and thirty feet, and visibility dropped to zero at times in squalls. The *Lloyd Bermuda*, some 200 miles east of Atlantic City and 160 miles south of Nantucket, had deviated from its course to Bermuda to ride directly into the three-story-high waves.

Then a sixty-foot breaking wave crashed on the port bow, washing four containers over the side. With the port side now forty tons lighter, the *Lloyd Bermuda* listed severely to starboard, bow down, and briefly reached a point of equilibrium. But then the starboard list continued and the entire ship quickly disappeared under the storm-tossed surface of the sea.

No more than five minutes elapsed from the time the wave struck until the ship sank. In this brutally fast disaster, eight of the eleven crewmen onboard died. Three were saved during daring rescues by a Coast Guard helicopter and a merchant ship that continued throughout the night as the gale raged.

Once details emerged, it appeared miraculous that anyone survived at all.

The first sign of trouble came at 7:10 PM when the Sandy Hook, New Jersey, Coast Guard station received a distress signal from the Cypriot-registered *Lloyd Bermuda*. "The captain said his cargo had shifted and he was capsizing," says Petty Officer Gregory Creedon, a spokesman for the First Coast Guard District in Boston. The captain gave the ship's approximate position as 38 degrees north latitude and 70 degrees west longitude, nearly one-third of the way to Bermuda. In his final transmission, the captain said, "The crew is abandoning ship."

Later, a more complete story of the tragedy was pieced together by Lieutenant Commander Theo Moniz, chief of inspection and investigation for the Coast Guard's Marine Safety Office in Providence, Rhode Island. Moniz prepared a report on the sinking of the *Lloyd Bermuda* for the government of Cyprus. In his investigation, Moniz spoke with the three survivors: Boatswain Dario Rene Masisa Lopez, thirty-five, of Honduras; crewman Jorge Umberto Montoya, thirty-one, of Guatemala; and Chief Engineer Asmi Anwar, thirty-eight, of Indonesia. While none of the survivors spoke English, Lopez gave the most comprehensive account.

On the sixteen-year-old *Lloyd Bermuda*, the house was

located aft behind the cargo hold and the engine room was below the house. The boat deck was one level up from the main deck; on the port and starboard sides of the house on the boat deck were both a life raft and lifeboat.

The life rafts were designed to be deployed in one of two methods, according to international requirements. One method is called "float-free," meaning the life raft is contained within a structure or nest. If the vessel sinks, it is designed to float out of this protective framework to the surface. In the second method the life raft is held in a cradle by banding straps, and one of the straps' ends is held in place by a hydrostatic release. When the vessel sinks and reaches a depth of some 30 feet, the hydrostatic release is triggered and the life raft floats to the surface. The method of inflation with both types is the same: A line on the vessel going down trips the carbon dioxide canisters.

In the case of the *Lloyd Bermuda*, one of the life rafts was inflated, but, said Moniz, it appeared to have been lashed down, "which would have defeated the purpose of a hydrostatic release or float-free release."

Lopez told Moniz that he was standing on the port side of the deck when the killer wave crashed down on the deck. He watched the four containers wash over the side. "The vessel took an immediate starboard list and a noticeable trim down in the bow," said Moniz. Lopez went to his room and put on his life jacket. Then he went to the port lifeboat deck. By the time he got there, he realized the starboard boat deck was already underwater. It would have been futile at that point to release the lifeboat on the port side as it would have crashed onto the deck.

Before Lopez could launch the life raft he had to wait for another crewman to get out of the way. In trying to get clear, this crewman fell overboard and disappeared. Moniz says that "Lopez, meanwhile, became entangled with another rope, which went around his torso; the bight of the rope trapped his leg. While several others were trying to untangle him, the vessel sank."

Lopez found himself in the water tied to the sinking ship. "Being a good boatswain, he had a knife and cut himself free as he was being dragged underwater," Moniz noted.

The Coast Guard dispatched two helicopters and a twin-engine jet from Otis Air National Guard Base on Cape Cod, a C-130 long-range search plane from Elizabeth City, North Carolina, and the cutter *Tamaroa* from Portsmouth, New Hampshire. Several merchant ships at sea as well as other military craft also joined in the search.

The five-man crew of the first of the big HH-3F Sikorsky helicopters sent from Otis was in the on-duty lounge when the call came. The helicopter was fueled and airborne in twenty minutes. After a two-and-a-half-hour flight to the scene of the accident, the crew searched for forty minutes before having to return to Nantucket to refuel. By the time they returned to the scene it was 3:00 AM and conditions were improving as the front moved out. Shafts of moonlight were breaking through the clouds and visibility had improved from zero to thirty feet to a few miles.

Petty Officer Randy Reed, the electronics engineer, was sweeping the searchlight back and forth across the water when he spotted the glint of reflective tape from a life jacket.

"It was literally a needle in a haystack, dumb luck. The light is a bright dot on the water that is 30 feet across. There's a little halo around it and beyond that pitch blackness," said Lieutenant (j.g.) Paul Ratte, the copilot. "We came back around to the same spot. Randy looked again. And I'll be darned, there's a guy sitting there in the water."

Petty Officer Joe Rock, twenty-four, the rescue swimmer, gave his equipment a final check. He wore a custom-fit drysuit designed for the Coast Guard rescue swimmers and a mask, fins, and snorkel. Using a winch, Petty Officer John Salmi, twenty-three, the flight mechanic, lowered Rock into the water in a survivor's sling, a three-foot square basket.

The Coast Guard rescue swimmers, also called survival men, actually are trained by the United States Navy, although the program now is used primarily by the Coast Guard itself. The Navy started training the helicopter swimmers in the 1960s during the Vietnam war. "A lot of Navy pilots ejected over water," says Rock, "but because of their injuries they couldn't crawl into the rescue devices that then were being lowered from helicopters. So the Navy trained people to go into the water to pull them out. Now it's become a fine art."

In the water, Rock disconnected himself from the sling and swam fifteen yards to the survivor, later identified as Lopez. He had been in the forty-five-degree water for nearly nine hours.

"He was severely hypothermic and in a state of shock," said Rock. "He was oblivious to what was going on around him. A survivor usually will turn his back to the helicopter because it kicks up quite a bit of spray. This guy didn't. He just sat there, holding onto this wood. He had tied himself, using the strings on his life jacket, to several fifteen-foot pieces of two-by-fours."

Working in the light of the one million-candlepower

beam from the helicopter, Rock first cut the lines holding Lopez to the wood. But he couldn't convince him to let go. Rock said he yelled at Lopez over the cold, howling gale, " 'Let go of that wood. You're okay now. Let's go in the helicopter.' No matter what I said, he wouldn't let go. I tried to pull him away from it, but he had a deathlike grip on it." Rock also didn't know how long the helicopter could stay on the scene, adding, "I thought if I didn't get this wood away from this guy, we're both going to be out here."

Rock grabbed Lopez's arm with one hand and the wood with the other and pulled them apart. But when Rock freed one hand, Lopez would grab at the wood with the other.

"Once I got that wood away from him, I was a lot happier. At that point, I was getting pretty tired," says Rock. The two were riding the large seas up and down. "You're trained to pull the survivor into the wave and have the wave break over your head rather than into your face," Rock says. "Even though I was doing that, it didn't make much difference. The waves were coming from everywhere. The wind just blew the tops of the waves off."

While Rock was in the water, the pilot, Lieutenant Commander Kevin Marshall, was trying to keep the helicopter hovering above him, not an easy task at night in high seas and a gale. "At night you have nothing to base your depth perception on," says Ratte. "So when we put a swimmer in the water, we'll put out two smoke floats. With the two lights floating on the water, you can give yourself an artificial depth perception as to how you're moving. We didn't want to risk losing sight of the survivor so we only tossed out one smoke. That made holding our position in the helicopter very difficult. It wasn't so bad once we got PO Rock in the water. Then we could move away and see him, and judge pretty much where we were. But it gets difficult when you have to pick him up."

Wave height was another problem. The helicopter's altimeter bounces a signal to the surface and back up. Thus, even if the helicopter was steady, the altimeter's pointer was going up and down twenty-five feet with each passing wave. "Obviously you couldn't get down so low that the seas would come up and smack the helicopter, but we also didn't want to be so high that you had the swimmer dangling seventy-five feet in the air," says Ratte. "We were trying to stay twenty-five to thirty feet above the waves, riding up and down above them trying to maintain a constant distance."

When Rock signaled for a pickup, the helicopter moved in and Salmi lowered the basket. "They would put the basket in the water and all of a sudden the wave would drop and the basket would now be in the air," says Rock. "And when the basket was in the water, the waves would throw it all about. It took us several attempts. The wind, meanwhile, was throwing the helicopter all around."

Rock helped Lopez into the basket until it became stable enough to hoist up. Once the basket was in the helicopter Lopez wouldn't let go of it. Salmi then quickly lowered a bare hook to Rock and winched him up on his rescue harness.

On board, no sooner had Rock and Reed removed Lopez from the basket than Salmi spotted another person in the water. Rock again went down and swam to him. "He had a severe head injury. He wasn't responding to me and he was floating with his head half in the water," he says.

At this time the current had placed Rock and the second crewman, who was naked except for his life jacket, into a position dangerously close to a large freighter that also had heard the *Lloyd Bermuda*'s distress call and had steamed over to help. After the freighter moved away, the helicopter moved back in and picked up the second crewman and later Rock. The second crewman, though, had no signs of life. (He was later pronounced dead on arrival at Falmouth Hospital in Falmouth, Massachusetts.)

Rock, who was also the medical technician on board in addition to serving as the rescue swimmer, directed his attention to Lopez. The survivor was so severely hypothermic that he had stopped shivering; his body temperature was down to about 88 degrees. He was stripped of his wet clothing and placed in a thermal recovery capsule, a sheepskin-lined bag that takes moisture away from the body and helps regenerate heat. Rock asked for a volunteer to get in the bag with Lopez to help rewarm him. Reed volunteered, stripped down to his underwear, and got in the bag with Lopez.

Rock, who has been in the Coast Guard for five years, says, "You can't warm a severely hypothermic person too quickly. If you do, you risk what is called afterdrop. This is when cold blood from the extremities rushes back to the heart and sends the heart into defibrillation. A person then can go out on you very quickly, so you have to rewarm him slowly.

"One of the important things about a survivor in that condition," Rock says, "is that even though he might not see you, his sense of hearing is the last thing to go. So I told Randy to sing to him and talk to him to maintain his level of consciousness and keep his spirits up." While Reed sang Billy Idol songs, Rock monitored Lopez's airway, pulse, and respiration on the two-and-a-half-hour trip to the hospital.

Chief Engineer Anwar's exit from the *Lloyd Bermuda*'s engine room was another incredible stroke of luck. Moniz says Anwar was in his room and didn't know a mishap had occurred until he heard the general alarm. He put on his life jacket and went to the bridge. The master directed Anwar to pump out the starboard ballast tanks in an attempt to decrease the list. Anwar went to the engine room and had the engineers on watch initiate the deballasting process. Once he saw it was under way, he went to the main deck, port side, in an attempt to leave the engine room. He found his way blocked due to water pressure.

Anwar turned around, Moniz says, "and saw water flooding into the back of the engine room and filling it. He was swept around the engine room, banging into various objects. Then he found himself underwater and rising rapidly. He came to the surface with the vessel gone. Somehow, he had been flushed out of the engine room."

On the surface, Anwar was pounded by what he believed were sixty-foot waves and howling winds. After approximately half an hour, a life ring surfaced next to him. Next to that surfaced a water light. He put his head and arms through the ring and tied the water light to him. After another hour, he heard three shipmates hollering. Anwar swam to them. His was the only light—the light spotted by the *M. V. Eagle*, a merchant ship, after they had spent six and a half hours in the water. The crew of the ship rescued Anwar and Montoya, but another crewman lost his grip on the rescue line and slipped away, disappearing in the seas. The fourth crewman, possibly disoriented due to ingesting seawater, had decided thirty minutes before the *Eagle* arrived to remove his life jacket and swim for shore. Moments later he had vanished under the waves.

As for Montoya, Moniz says, "No matter where I took him in the scenario, he just said he went into the water. It made a lasting impression on him."

Montoya and Anwar were transferred from *Eagle* to the *Tamaroa*, which took them to Woods Hole on Cape Cod. They were then treated and released from Falmouth Hospital.

The question remained as to why the *Lloyd Bermuda* sank and sank so quickly. In addition to the sixty-nine containers on board, the ship carried nine tons of steel pipe and two 4,800 pound Bobcats—four-wheeled, tractorlike machines slightly smaller than a forklift. The steel-hulled vessel had only one-container-height storage on deck.

The ship did reach a point of equilibrium and then the fatal starboard list continued. That can be caused by taking on more water over the top and having the hull completely open, or by structural failure below the waterline, allowing water to come in. The survivors indicated the ship did not take water on over the topsides.

"I suspect some kind of below-the-waterline damage," said Moniz.

There was no way, though, for the crew to check the condition of the hull. There was no way to go forward belowdecks, only on deck. Because of the storm, no one could have gone forward on deck. And from the bridge, there was no way to see the forward portion of the ship due to the configuration of the containers. "Looking down, you couldn't see the deck the containers were lashed to," said Moniz.

While Moniz compiled the data, the survivors headed home. Before Lopez left the hospital to return to his wife and child in Honduras, he received a visit from the helicopter crew. "He didn't recognize any of us when we walked into the room," says Rock. "He didn't even recognize me and we were face-to-face in the water under the bright searchlight. But the minute Randy started speaking, he remembered his voice."

March, 1989

⚓

NOWHERE TO HIDE

A sixty-five-foot Donzi sportfisherman takes on a 110-miles-per-hour hurricane 300 miles offshore, and wins—and then loses.

BY JOHN CLEMANS

"If I got greedy and put it up to 900 rpm we'd slam off the last wave and get creamed by the next one. The banging was so violent I had big bruises on the backs of my legs. Every third wave I was taking green water on the bridge. Then it got worse. By nine o'clock the bridge had been flooded so often that the laser plotter shorted out and the electrical panel next to me caught fire. Flames were on my left and green water was washing over me as I held onto the wheel with both hands. 'Wait a minute,' I said, 'there's something wrong with this picture,'" Bill Holekamp, owner of the Donzi 65 sportfisherman *Oasis*, remembers.

We're besieged by pictures. They inform our sense of the world and of ourselves. They let us relive past pleasures and pain and the experiences of others. When Hurricane Andrew hit the Atlantic coast in August it was pictured on TV. We saw its bow—trees swaying, homes being secured; and we saw its wake—trees gone, homes gutted. But the middle was curiously missing.

When Hurricane Darby hit *Oasis* in the Pacific in July, it too was recorded on video, and the footage is much the same. There's a tape of it—but the middle is missing.

The tape shows men fishing. It begins in Manzanillo on Mexico's west coast. *Oasis* sits majestically at Las Hadas, perennial hangout of the rich and famous. The men sit around a table. They smugly exult in the good times they're having. The date on the screen is July 1.

There's a beautiful girl on the beach. There are scenes of preparation: filling bladder tanks, loading a Whaler and two personal watercraft on the bow. Then there's a sunset, and islands in the distance, followed by fishing. There are sailfish, there are wahoo, there are tuna. There's blue water and blue sky. The date is July 3.

Watching the men fishing and having fun on video with the knowledge of what is to come provides an eerie echo of the hidden backbeat of life—how we all get up in the morning oblivious to impending catastrophe.

The fishing footage is extraordinary. Billfish leap all over the place. A blue marlin thrashes wildly across the transom, knocking the top of the fish door open. Sailfish are tagged, tuna are taken. More tags and toasts and arms draped around shoulders in group shots of glory. The boat looks strong and handsome. The date is July 4.

Suddenly the screen is gray: The sky is light gray; the water is dark gray. And it's rough. The men are inside the cabin, sprawled on the settee, smiling but not happy. The picture bounces. A shot from the cockpit shows the wake being devoured by the seething sea before it can even begin to form.

Then the only outside view is from inside. The gray shape of an island is barely visible through rattling Levolor blinds, a spray-splattered window and airborne water. The men are in life jackets. Huge waves wash past. One wave is bigger than the rest. It explodes against the glass.

"What was that?" someone asks. The camera records upside down. It captures overturned chairs. . . .

The next shot on the video is of bananas being loaded on a freighter at night. The lights above the vast covered berth are a frigid shade of green.

"That first wave knocked us down," says Bill Holekamp. "The second one knocked us out."

The second wave came eight hours after the first. Between them is an eternity of "adventure," unrecorded by the camera, that is every boater's worst nightmare. Bill Holekamp ended up in the wrong place at the wrong time and had to take his boat through a 110-mile-per-hour hurricane.

His boat, *Oasis,* was new. He had only fished aboard her for seven days during the delivery trip she was on from Fort Lauderdale, Florida, to his home on Naples Bay near Long Beach, California. With Holekamp were four friends. Also aboard were a captain and mate. Their route from Manzanillo to Cabo San Lucas, at the tip of Baja California, included the Revillagigedo Islands, a fifty-mile long chain 300 miles offshore, where the fishing is phenomenal.

When *Oasis* left its anchorage off San Benedicto, the northernmost island, at dawn on July 5, bound for Cabo San Lucas, the sea was rough. Yet Holekamp continued on. His most recent weather update, relayed by a boat in Cabo from a weatherfax, indicated a storm 400 miles to the south moving north at 10 miles per hour.

Why worry? At the Donzi 65's cruising speed of 30 knots, even in six-foot seas, *Oasis* did not seem at risk. One of the reasons Holekamp had decided to buy a Donzi Z-65 was the boat's strength. Bob Roscioli, who builds the sixty-five-footer, believes in overbuilding it. If Holekamp were going to be caught 300 miles offshore in a major storm, at least he had faith that he was on the right boat. He also had faith in the weather info he'd received the night before, but that turned out to be a big mistake.

"Don't rely on a weatherfax when it comes to hurricanes," he advises. "Weatherfaxes can be six hours old, and hurricanes can change speed in a hurry."

Hurricane Darby swept up the Mexican coast and veered out to sea in a path that took it directly over the Revillagigedo Islands. With the wind and seas building as *Oasis* slogged on toward Cabo San Lucas, Holekamp began to have misgivings. He called his contacts in Cabo for a weather update, and learned that the storm to the south had become a hurricane with sustained winds of 90 to 100 knots, and that its speed was 19 to 20 miles per hour, rather than 10 miles per hour as the last report had indicated. He was 30 miles north of San Benedicto in fifteen-foot seas and was making only 10 knots.

What to do? Keep running north in hopes that Darby would turn westward (as such storms normally do) and that *Oasis* would escape the worst of the storm's northern edge? Or turn back and hope that the Revillagigedos could offer some protection?

"It was an interesting call," says Holekamp. "If we had kept going and the storm had kept heading north, it would have hit us full force about 100 miles off the middle of nowhere."

He decided to turn back, even though it meant heading

directly into the hurricane: "We figured it was going to catch us one way or the other, so we decided to go for the protection—the lee of San Benedicto." Except there was no lee. . . .

Oasis reversed course at about 11:00 AM. The seas were approaching twenty feet, and the wind drove the spray so fiercely and unrelentingly that diving masks were needed on the bridge.

The hoped-for relief from eight-mile-long San Benedicto was nonexistent. The south end of the island, which seemed to offer slightly calmer conditions from afar, turned out to be even more hellacious than the north end, and "inshore" was unapproachable because of the confusion of the waves and currents and the risk of losing power and being washed against the lava cliffs.

"The waves just seemed to sweep around the island from both directions," says Holekamp. They "ventured" around the island with large amounts of pumice blowing off the volcanic rock. "We had a gritty feeling between our teeth and in our noses," reports Hal Neibling, one of the four guests on board.

San Benedicto has virtually no beach, and reaching the island by life raft seemed suicidal. The Donzi's bow was buried in oncoming waves, but the boat was holding its own. The only feasible option was to wait out the storm on the west side of the island. Says Holekamp, "We had plenty of fuel and we could trade watches and keep the engines running through the night. I think we would have been okay, except that at two in the afternoon a huge rogue wave came out of nowhere and just creamed us."

This was "the first wave," the wave that ended the on-board video. It engulfed *Oasis* as if she were a toy boat in a bathtub when a child suddenly stands up. The wave ripped the Boston Whaler and the two PWCs off the bow and washed over the flying bridge. It killed the starboard engine and shorted out the electric throttle controls and most of the communications equipment. "It takes a lot to stop a diesel," muses Holekamp. "The impact alone wouldn't have done it. I don't know what did it, but in a single stroke we were down to one engine in forward idle, and we could no longer hold our position."

Dave Friedenberg, director of engineering at Florida Detroit Diesel-Allison, speculates that enough water came through the air vents to momentarily smother the starboard 16V-92TA DDEC engine. Later, the starboard-side air vents were found to be missing.

With no throttle, no forward/reverse, and only one engine, *Oasis* was off on a wild ride. There was nowhere to go but downsea and nothing to do but try to keep the boat from turning sideways. Waves bombarded the cockpit, washing gear overboard, and within no time *Oasis*— surfing northwest at about 10 miles per hour—was almost as far from San Benedicto as she'd been five hours earlier.

Darby had reached cruising altitude: Winds held at over 100 miles per hour and seas assumed a baseline of thirty feet. "We feared for our lives, our boat, and our survival," is how Hal Neibling describes the prevailing mood on board.

In retrospect, Holekamp considers the Donzi's performance extraordinary: "I was able to keep the boat pointed in the right direction at only 900 rpm. How many other boats could have done that on one engine?" It was when the waves started filling the cockpit that tracking became more difficult. "The cockpit started taking waves that would have sunk most other boats. It was full to the brim three times," says Holekamp.

In an attempt to turn the bow into the waves, the sea anchor was deployed. It was about as effective as using an umbrella as a parachute. "Don't leave home on a boat this size without a fifteen-foot sea anchor with at least 300 feet of line," cautions Holekamp. "We had a seven-footer."

Captain Lance Ekberg, from Huntington Beach, California, and mate Jay Halford, turned the helm over to Holekamp and headed for the engine room—their new home. While Holekamp, dreading the moment the steering system would lose the wrestling match he was having with the wheel, tried to keep *Oasis* from broaching using only the rudders, the crew attempted to revive the flattened propulsion system.

Just before dark—when things looked the bleakest, and Holekamp was lowering life raft canisters from the bridge and chucking $1,000 fishing rigs overboard because they were in the way—Ekberg and Halford were able to hot-wire the starboard engine and reestablish forward throttle control, giving *Oasis* a fighting chance once again. But within the hour the starboard engine was back on the canvas. The boat was doomed to fight with one bruised hand: portside power in forward gear.

Oasis responded surprisingly well to her new situation: Holekamp was able to turn the bow into the sea and inch back toward San Benedicto. At 875 rpm he could make one-and-a-half knots. He could hold the semblance of a heading when he could read the compass through his dive mask.

But it was hard to judge whether *Oasis* was winning or losing, especially from Holekamp's vantage point. The sea

seemed vertical. Every third wave was washing over the
bridge. And it was at about this time that a fire flared up
to Holekamp's left from the short-circuited electrical
panel.

Then, around 10 PM, the *second* devastating wave hit
Oasis. This one came from the side and shattered the salon's starboard windows. "All of a sudden everyone in the
salon was on the bridge saying, 'Bill, we're getting off
now.' They were ready to bail out," says Holekamp. Mike
Thomas's arm was badly cut. The wave had dumped three
feet of water in the salon, and when the water washed
against the electrical panel, "it looked like *Star Wars*. We
could feel a current of electricity up to our knees," recounts Neibling.

Rick Macklin, another of Holekamp's fishing buddies,
had just stretched out on the settee to pray when the
windows went. "As we all went underwater in the salon,
we thought the boat had turned upside down and we
were going to the bottom," he says.

The wave blew out the salon door and cascaded into
the cockpit and down into the engine room, where Ekberg
and Halford were already knee-deep in water from the
blown starboard air vents and were being treated to their
own version of *Star Wars* as they tried to rewire the bilge
pumps directly to the batteries.

The generator and 12-volt system were now dead, but
the 24-volt system held, which kept the radar going.
"That was lucky," says Holekamp, "because without the
radar we'd have never found the island—or we might
have found it when we didn't want to. . . ."

The boat was being thrown around so violently that
within one sweep of the radar, the island would change
position 90 degrees on the screen. To see the overhead

radar screen, Rick Macklin had to crouch behind the helm console and look straight up as Holekamp steered and Ed Ragone, the fourth guest, watched for breaking waves.

With just one engine; with water up to the shaft coupling, which spewed it around like a lawn sprinkler; with water in the Racors filters; with a fried electrical system with virtually every built-in appliance ripped from its moorings; with the batteries underwater; and with just a handheld ICOM VHF operational, *Oasis* pounded back toward San Benedicto—pounded so hard that the toilet in the master head split in half. But she endured, reaching the island by 3:00 AM.

The first Mayday had been sent out via single-sideband twelve hours earlier, and the nearest Coast Guard C-130 Hercules had been dispatched from Sacramento—2,000 miles away. It circled *Oasis* most of the night at 4,000 feet, offering some comfort, but little help.

During the predawn hours of July 6 *Oasis* waited in the lee of San Benedicto. The storm had diminished and a 476-foot freighter, the *Chiquita Roma*, had been persuaded by the Coast Guard to turn back to Cabo San Lucas. When it arrived at midday, *Oasis* had to move offshore and the seven men had to attempt boarding the freighter in ten-foot seas. Having survived their thirty-hour ordeal aboard the Donzi, they now faced the dangerous maneuver of getting off onto a cargo net and rope ladders as *Oasis* banged against the side of the *Chiquita Roma*.

"Our starboard side crashed into the rolling ship and was further damaged with no chance for anyone to get off. We all feared being hit by flying fiberglass and antennae or being crushed between the vessels with the twenty-foot rolling and heaving," says Hal Neibling.

Extra lines were lowered and attached to *Oasis*'s bow and stern cleats and the men made mad leaps for the ladders. Holekamp's head was nearly crushed, but they all made it onto "the best cruise ship we'd ever been on."

The hero of this tale is the boat. The 65-foot Donzi sportfisherman had done exactly what Bob Roscioli had built it to do—it had weathered conditions far beyond the call of duty. It had taken on seas as high as forty feet and winds well over 100 miles per hour with just one of its two engines running. Hurricane Darby was the ultimate sea trial. Such conditions are rarely, if ever, encountered in a lifetime of boating, and Roscioli could only believe his boats could survive them. Now he *knows* they can.

Oasis had actually come through relatively unscathed. There were no cracks in the hull or bulkheads, and the engines and generator remained solidly mounted. The bow pulpit was undamaged and the anchors in place. The large etched-glass aft window in the salon came through uncracked, which indicates a minimal amount of "racking." The heavy-duty bilge pumps had proven their worth. Holekamp, who has owned several other boats, is convinced that if it weren't for Roscioli's insistence on structural strength and on doing everything "right," he'd be dead today.

The boat had won, but in the end it lost. Having been through such a traumatic experience and thankful he and everyone else aboard were still alive, Holekamp was unwilling to let the crew remain aboard to try to reach a safe harbor. Consequently, so as not to be a hazard to navigation, the sea strainers were broken and *Oasis* was left to sink.

Bill Holekamp loves to fish. He had a close call and lost his boat, but he figures that his share of bad luck is now behind him. The blue water beckons, and he's determined to get back offshore. In what? Why, another Donzi 65, of course.

January, 1993

⚓

CRASH

At 95 miles per hour, Cigarette Racing Team's forty-two-foot raceboat hits a wave off Japan and does a barrel-roll with the author still on board.

BY CRAIG BARRIE

In eleven years of racing, I've done a lot of things with boats. I've had them up on their sides, I've stuffed them, I've had them trip; but other than being a little sore, I've never gotten injured in one. Until this time.

It all began routinely enough. I was in Japan with the Cigarette Racing Team to compete in the twenty-fourth Atami Ocean Cup, the final race of the Japanese Offshore Grand Prix. On the day before the race, we walked into the "dry-pit" area of the venue in Atami, Japan, where the boats sat on their trailers, to check on our chief rival in the Superboat Class, the Kazuma Factory team with its fifty-foot Cougar catamaran. The team members seemed more serious about winning than ever. They had invited Steve and Clive Curtis, the owners of Cougar Marine in England, to Japan to watch the race.

We put our forty-two-foot, V-bottom Cigarette Revolution 188 race boat *Mr. Cigarette* in the water for a test run, heading out into the ocean, which is known to be rough here. We monitored the gauges as we increased the speed of its three 1,000-horsepower Hawk engines up to 100 miles per hour. At that point, the boat made a hard turn to starboard. Apparently there was something loose in the steering. So we went back to the pits to make the necessary repairs.

That evening we enjoyed some fresh fish, and were entertained by my father, George Barrie, who had come along on this trip. In addition to being the founder of Fabergé Perfumes and producer and songwriter for seven movies, including *Touch of Class* (he's received three Academy Award nominations), he is also master of the one-liner.

Race day arrived, made even more exciting by the addition of 40,000 spectators. Before putting our life jackets and helmets on, we did press interviews. The major question was, "Will *Mr. Cigarette*, having won two races already, make it three in a row and sweep the Japanese Grand Prix series?"

As we drove the boat out to the milling area before the race, we felt confident and nervous at the same time. I thought of my father, who had asked me if we were going to win—or had he made this long journey for nothing? Then the pace boat raised the green flag. We accelerated, and were the first boat into Turn One. As we made the long run toward the second marker, the *Kazuma Factory* Superboat, along with two other catamarans that were Open Class contenders, *K. E. Marine* and a Jaguar cat, pulled alongside us. We settled into fourth place.

As we turned left into the second lap, the wave pattern became erratic. The waves ranged from two-footers to six-footers, with a rolling sea. Then *Kazuma Factory* threw a blade off its propeller and cut the steering hose. This happened about a quarter-mile in front of us. I remember thinking that with all the preparations they had made, this team would not be especially happy to see *Mr. Cigarette* go by.

Now we were in third place overall, and first in the Superboat Class. We ran the rest of the laps in head-to-head competition with the Jaguar and *K. E. Marine*.

Offshore racing in Japan is based on the number of laps you complete in a certain time period. This race was ninety minutes long. On our fourteenth lap, we passed the finish line at one hour, twenty-nine minutes and twenty-two seconds, which meant it was necessary to go around again. At this point, as the race was about to end, there seemed to be a lot of non-race boat traffic. Also, a ferryboat called *Seagow*, which takes tourists between the mainland and a resort island, had passed by the race course. This ferry is a catamaran, probably a 100-footer, and throws a giant wake. I'm sure that part of the accident was due to that wake, although *Seagow* went by us well before it happened.

As we kept running, the Jaguar was maybe six boat lengths in front of us on our starboard side. We were doing approximately 95 miles per hour and were catching up to the thirty-five-foot cat. We were bouncing a little bit more than usual because we were almost out of fuel. Two helicopters buzzed around us, filming the finish.

We caught air a couple of times and the boat kind of prop-walked for a second, and dropped her nose down. I picked it right back up again with the throttles and we were still in the chase. About three boat lengths away, I saw the Jaguar hit something and take a nice leap. We were in a position to pass when *Mr. Cigarette* hit this wave in a semi-quartering sea.

She pulled her nose way up and kept climbing. As she got up in the air, she started to kite and cock a little bit to her starboard side. And then as she settled back down, she tripped over the wave, her nose tucked in, hooked to the left, and then she barrel-rolled herself over.

Bud Lorow, our technical engineer, and Scott Layman, who was driving, were tossed out of the boat on the starboard side. Hideo Mizuno, in the back, was tossed out also.

When the boat hooked, she pushed me down inside my bolster as she started to roll over. I remember looking out the side of the boat and seeing the reflection of *Mr. Cigarette* and the number *24* on the water. At that point, my left hand was outside the boat holding onto the cleat, while my other hand was on the throttles. I had my helmet's full face shield open just a touch so I could see out, because it had been blurred by mist during the race. As the boat rolled over, the water hit my face and tore off the shield.

The next thing I remember, I was upside down, thrown into the water or sucked out of the bolster into the water. By the time I reached the surface, *Mr. Cigarette* was bow-up and was submerged from the console back. She looked like a buoy, bobbing up and down in the sea.

Scott and Bud were swimming toward me. I only knew this now because I've seen it on videotape. When they reached me, they told me I looked fine and that the rescue boat was on its way (that was half a lie). It reached us in ten or twelve minutes.

The rescue boat's crewmen brought me in like they were landing a sailfish or marlin. They propped me up against the ladder that goes to the flying bridge. I knew something was very wrong because I couldn't move my left arm. It was just lying on top of my thigh. I didn't know then that my shoulder was dislocated. We ran quickly back to the port, where an ambulance was waiting to take me to the hospital.

There, they X-rayed me and hoisted me onto a table, then gave me a shot that immediately knocked me out. Scott said that the doctor jumped up onto the table, put his right foot in my armpit, took his hand, and with a golf-swing motion, popped my shoulder back in place.

When they revived me a few minutes later, my father had just arrived. With tears in his eyes, he gave me a hug and a kiss and asked if I was okay. Upon my saying yes, he said, "You know, living can be hazardous to your health."

Bud, Scott, and Mizuno were really lucky. Scott, although sore, was out running around Japan that night. Mizuno was in semi-shock and Bud had a couple of broken ribs and cartilage damage in his chest.

I had a dislocated shoulder with a fractured bone, four broken ribs, a black eye, a cut over my eye and nose; I'd bitten my tongue, and my left arm was 95 percent paralyzed between my elbow and fingertips, requiring many hours of painful therapy. Other than that, I felt great.

We still had completed enough laps to win our class, so *Mr. Cigarette* was undefeated in three starts—and was the Japanese Grand Prix Superboat winner. She was towed back to the pits. Her transom was damaged and the engine room hatch was gone. The motors were intact.

Performance boating is a serious sport, be it for pleasure or racing. These boats can do some crazy things when you get them into trouble. They can trip and stuff, kite and flip, hook and roll, or any combination thereof. I look at the video of the race and say, "it's not an airplane," but the boat took off like one. Between launching, tripping, stuffing, hooking, and rolling, we did everything.

I called it the "Great El-Rollo," after watching boogie-boarding on TV. These guys call it an "El-Rollo" when they roll the boogie board 360 degrees and keep going. So far I have only done a half El-Rollo. That's enough.

I've been asked many times if I will continue racing, and the answer is *yes*. My friends say that during my racing career I've done some spectacular aerobatics and that I've been very lucky. Well, I feel very lucky today because I'm here to tell the story. And the most delightful part of the story is, we won!

November, 1991

⚓

TALL SHIP TRAGEDY

When the 117-foot barque Marques *sinks off Bermuda, she takes nineteen crewmembers with her.*

BY BONNIE WAITZKIN

A brisk 25-mile-per-hour wind and splashing seas drowned out the triumphant band music from a nearby sightseeing boat as the 117-foot barque *Marques* crossed the starting line to join the parade of thirty-nine tall ships racing from Bermuda to Halifax, Nova Scotia. A three-masted square-rigger built at Valencia in 1917, the *Marques* carried square sheets from the fore- and mainmast and gaff-sail on the mizzen. As she headed out to sea, the sun shone on her flax canvases billowing out eighty-eight feet above the water like an antique patchwork quilt. Her broad-beamed hull rhythmically sank from view in the trough, but the fleet never lost sight of the twenty-seven-foot bowsprit, set at a jaunty upward angle that somehow gave her the look of a gargantuan billfish.

The *Marques* and her youthful crew had just won the San Juan to Bermuda leg of the Cutty Sark Tall Ships

Race and the ship carried the tasteful Bermuda trophy—
a mariner's clock set under a sterling model of Sir Francis
Drake's *Golden Hind*—in her spacious captain's cabin
under the poop deck. In this 800-mile race to Halifax, the
Marques was the boat to beat.

Half of the *Marques*'s twenty-eight-person crew on this
leg of the race were between fifteen and twenty-five years
old, many of them aspiring sailors who had only stepped
aboard a tall ship for the first time the day before, at the
quay in Hamilton. The Sail Training Association, a twenty-
eight-year-old British organization, and its American
counterpart, ASTA, sponsor the Tall Ships Races to match
old sailing vessels with inexperienced young crews in
never-to-be-forgotten, sail-your-heart-out ocean crossings
guaranteed to teach seamanship and build character. The
association tries to select trainees from across a wide social
spectrum. The father of one *Marques* crew member, a high
school dropout, said of his son, "I'm sending a very trou-
bled boy. I hope he grows up at sea."

The permanent *Marques* crew were bare-chested, barefoot twentieth-century buccaneers. Their fingers were cal-
lused from splicing hemp and manilla; each carried a knife
at his belt and sported some distinguishing trinket—a
beaded bracelet, a gold earring, or a shark's tooth pen-
dant—like characters out of a Robert Louis Stevenson
novel. The young trainees quickly assumed the look and
mannerisms of the *Marques*'s permanent crew. But their
novice standing was betrayed by bandages around toes
ripped open climbing rigging, or by their imprecise use of
newly learned nautical terms. On the *Marques*, pretending
to be a seasoned sailor was part of the process of actually
becoming one.

By evening of the first day out of Hamilton, Saturday,

June 2, most of the trainees aboard the *Marques* were seasick as the barque rhythmically seesawed over waves
building to twelve feet. The sky blackened, and only the
hardiest of the newcomers joined the crew at watch. Captain Stuart Finlay ordered the royals, the gallants, the top-
gallants, the royal staysail, the flying jib, the spanker, and
the main course down to give the trainees a comfortable
ride. Then he joined his Antiguan wife, Aloma, and
fifteen-month-old son, Christopher, who were sleeping in
the poop cabin.

All that starless night the wind blew steadily at Force
6. From time to time the watch noted the mast lights of
another tall ship to port or to starboard. At the 4:00 AM
watch change Andy "Sparks" Freeman, the ship's twenty-
two-year-old engineer, yielded the wheel to Phil Sefton,
twenty, of Cumbria, England. Sefton was tall, straight-
backed and blond-haired, cocky with youth and exuber-
ance. He had logged 10,000 nautical miles aboard the
Marques, and the planks under her helm were as familiar
to his feet as work shoes are to a city-dweller. Never had
Sefton felt the antique barque sail so splendidly fast and
true. Her course was 010 degrees on a port reach, with
the wind from the southwest. She was making more than
9 knots—good speed—despite full water and fuel tanks.
Her lee rail dipped occasionally under the waves. Sparks
lingered on the poop to admire the fine sail. Although he
had daytime duties as engineer, he had requested watch
duty because he considered it "good fun to watch with
the guys."

At 4:10 stars appeared and the wind slackened, as if the
sky were holding its breath. The sails, stretched open to
the southwest wind, relaxed slightly. The ship straightened, gently rolling the sleeping crew and passengers back

toward the center of their bunks. Then she sailed into rain. A few of those on deck but not on watch retreated to the companionway, remaining on call in case there was a change of sails. James McAleer, forty-seven, stayed on deck because he was seasick. Below, sixteen-year-old Clif McMillan, tired after his watch and wearing sweatpants and a flannel shirt, was preparing to climb into his bunk.

Suddenly a frightful wall of wind overtook the barque from the southwest. Paradoxically, this devastating blow from behind seemed to stop the unsuspecting ship in her tracks. A voice cried: "Veer off, veer off!" The blast knocked John "Jay" Ash, a twenty-three-year-old geology teacher and soccer coach at Trinity-Pawling School in Pawling, New York, down the companionway. Jay felt the boat stop and heel violently. The *Marques* paused first as if she might recover, then quietly lay down in the rough ocean without a fight. Everyone on deck was pitched to starboard. "All hands, all hands!" someone screamed.

Bill Barnhardt, a twenty-four-year-old art student from Pennsylvania, saw his watch leader slip out of sight over the rail. "Cut the sails loose," someone called into the roaring wind. Bill struggled to his feet, and now waist deep in water, climbed slipping and stumbling up the vertical deck to the port rail and hand over hand down from the poop. He felt no emotion except the urgent need to save himself, to save the ship.

The *Marques* now lay helplessly on her starboard side, her masts pointing on a 110 degree angle into the water, her open hatch filling as the waves swept against the deck. The only slim chance to save the ship was to cut loose the sails that were now dragging her under—a death ballast. Barnhardt gripped the rail with his left arm and slashed futilely at the thick halyards. Then the *Marques*'s rudder came out of the water. Barnhardt felt himself being pulled down with the ship. Underwater, he became tangled in the rigging he had been trying to cut. He started climbing the ropes to the surface but became disoriented, not sure which way was up. He had just seen the movie *An Officer and a Gentleman*, and a lifesaving scene flashed through his mind; he blew bubbles, and followed them to the surface.

The *Marques* was now riding with her bowsprit pointing to the bottom, her stern awash. The four-paned windows of the poop cabin, where Captain Finlay must have been struggling to get out with his wife and toddler son, were the last part of the *Marques* seen by those thrown overboard. One crewman, treading water, kept expecting Finlay to crash through the glass and escape.

Inside the sunken boat Ozzie Coles, a 19-year-old mason and one of the three Antiguans from the village of Willikies aboard, dove down through the water in the corridor past cabins to the main hatch. The hatch cover had slid shut when the boat heeled over. Coles pushed and pushed. He believed he was dead. Then the hatch moved and Coles squeezed through. He quickly surfaced.

Coles treaded water alone in the darkness, unable to see above waves cresting at twenty feet. He was shaken and frightened to the core by his near-drowning. Then salvation sprang from the *Marques* below in the form of a Viking life raft, hissing as it inflated. Dennis Ord swam to it and climbed in, then helped Coles aboard.

An itinerant seaman, Ord, at fifty-four, was the oldest crewman and first mate—a short, powerfully built man whose face was hidden by a fine gray beard, and whose nose and bald head were continually peeling from exposure to the sun. He was wearing foul weather gear when he was thrown overboard.

Ord gathered six men into the raft. Besides Coles there were Bobby Cooper, Bill Barnhardt, Clif McMillan, John Ash, and Phil Sefton. Ord calmed the six survivors by assuring them that the *Marques* was required to radio a report to the race command twice daily. When her call was missed, a search would begin. He collected all the knives to avoid accidentally puncturing the raft and opened the box of supplies. He had lost his glasses, so he had trouble reading labels and instructions.

The seven men were stunned and very cold. Coles, the Antiguan, was losing his color and approaching hypothermia. He was wearing only nylon shorts, a T-shirt and a windbreaker. The men huddled together for warmth, but Ord separated them to balance the raft. "You don't want to go over like the *Marques*," he said. The men were sure the ship had gone completely under.

Bobby Cooper, nineteen, a Scotsman who had been aboard two years, held Ord's legs while he stood outside the tentlike cover and fired off flares. When a second raft washed close by, Cooper swam to it with a safety line and secured it for use later.

Meanwhile, not far away, Sparks, the engineer, had clung to the steering-box cover until he had made it onto an inflated raft. Then he had immediately fired off a flare. In the distance he could see two other rafts bobbing in the raging sea; the *Marques* was completely gone. He quickly climbed under the raft hood and began bailing, dressed warmly in a wool jacket, boiler pants, and oilskins, but wet and cold nonetheless. He recalled stories about rafts splitting in half during the Fastnet disaster five years before. He repeatedly became seasick due to the pitching of the twenty-man raft.

To the north the *Smuga Cienna*, a Polish yawl built in

1972, spotted the flares. She was unable to come around in such a strong wind, but radioed a Mayday call. The *Zawisza Czarny*, a three-masted Polish schooner twenty-five miles to the north, took in her sails and changed course to respond. She saw thick clouds and lightning on the horizon. At 7:00 AM she spotted something orange in the water, a life raft. Then she saw two more tied together.

For some reason Sparks looked through the hatch, which he had closed hours before to keep out spray and wash. He saw the Polish schooner. "I can't describe how I felt," he said with a slight stutter. "Elated, I guess." After Sparks joined Ord and the others aboard, a Polish crewman pointed out a fin that had been following the raft.

After taking the eight men aboard, the schooner's Captain Jan Sauer began sending Mayday signals and continued to search. Crew members saw ladies' shoes, apples, tables, and other furniture float by, as well as three empty life jackets, a life ring with *Marques* printed on it, and an inflated dinghy. A helicopter joined the hunt and signaled the schooner toward a man afloat in a life vest. The *Zawisza Czarny* issued a lifeboat and found James McAleer, who had slept on deck because he had been seasick, dead. He must have been thrown against the mast or a railing because his face was smashed in. If he was lucky, he went overboard unconscious and drowned immediately.

The elegant American *Eagle*, a 295-foot square-rigged barque built in 1936 and carrying over 100 Coast Guard cadets, left the race to lead the search-and-rescue operation. Also searching were three Canadian frigates, the HMS *Skeena*, *Margaree* and *Assinboine;* a Canadian supply ship; an 800-foot tanker; United States Navy aircraft; and helicopters. The *Zawisza Czarny* turned back to Bermuda with the eight survivors.

The *Marques* and the 126-year-old *Cuidad de Inca*, the oldest wooden square-rigged sailing vessel afloat, were owned by British nationals Mark Litchfield and Robin Cecil-Wright and operated by the China Clipper Society, a nonprofit organization founded to keep the two museum pieces afloat. Expenses were paid by memberships, charters, and film productions. The *Marques* had played HMS *Beagle* in the BBC's *The Voyage of Charles Darwin* and *The China Cloud* in *Tai Pan*.

The *Inca*, a 125-foot brig, had been unable to start the race with the *Marques* on Saturday morning because of a bent pipe in her steering mechanism. Her crew was up early Sunday to finish repairs so they could join the race. At 8:20 an Antiguan trainee shouted down the hatch to Litchfield that there was radio traffic about the *Marques*.

The day to follow was a mal de mer of emotions for the *Inca*'s crew, many of whom had sailed on the *Marques* and considered her home. Rumors contradicted rumors. The first was that the *Marques* was down. "May God save and protect all those who were aboard *Marques* from the perils of the sea this day," one sailor wrote in his diary. Then reporters and camera crews began to appear on the Hamilton quay.

Hardy Le Bel, a sixteen-year-old trainee from Providence, Rhode Island, tried to contain his concern for his younger brother, Thomas, who had sailed on the *Marques*. To pass the time, Hardy and another trainee studied chart reading with an ASTA counselor. Then stories began to circulate that the *Marques* had been seen awash. Relief and exhilaration. The crew hoped their friends were still aboard. Next came reports of life rafts found, of eight rescued. Later an official report that Stu Gillespie had been picked up by the Canadian frigate *Assinboine*. Every rumor was given the most favorable interpretation. It was unthinkable that the *Marques* could have actually sunk.

At midnight, someone said they had talked to the *Marques* by radio hours after the alleged sinking. Litchfield immediately tried to confirm this, but without success. He reminded the crew of the *Marques*'s performance in high seas. Off the Balearic Islands under full sail she had taken gusts in excess of Force 12 winds, heeled over until the water was two feet above the port rail, and then stood back up again. *Inca* crewman Tina Rawnsley had been up the mast when she heeled over. "The sea was brushed flat by the wind," he recalled. "The *Marques* is strong." The crew's spirits brightened. They sang together until 2 AM.

But morning drowned all hopes. The eight survivors on the Zawisza Czarny had disembarked at St. George's and reported to police that the ship was lost.

Stateside the same anxious uncertainty prevailed. Clifton McMillan's father, Paul, an airline pilot, heard of the sinking while he was in the air. It was hours before he was able to call the Coast Guard to learn that his son was a survivor. In Bermuda, relatives of the missing began to gather and Bermudians opened their homes to accommodate them.

Dr. Paul Sheldon, the designated ship's doctor for the *Marques* and the *Inca*, spent time talking with the bereaved parents and with David Howel, whose thirty-seven-year-old wife, Sue, who taught celestial navigation at Mystic Seaport, had gone down with the ship. (They had three children.) "There is naturally a lot of denial and fantasy,"

Sheldon said. "They want to believe that there is still hope for their loved ones."

Mark Litchfield, like his father and grandfather, had been an officer in the Royal Navy. He told a friend, "I've often been overcome by a depressing reverie before falling asleep, where I imagine what goes on when a ship sinks and people can't get out. . . . When we bought the *Marques*, Robin fixed her up in Spain and then wrote to me to come navigate her back. In Gilbraltar we met another old Spanish ship that sailed ahead of us. She didn't make it. Her captain saw the ship go down with his wife and children trapped below.

"It's horrific—Finlay and the others," Litchfield continued, shifting restlessly on his chair. "I'm damn sure they're not going to be found. They were asleep and then plunging to the bottom with water bursting in everywhere like a ruptured submarine."

Tuesday afternoon the international press gathered at Malabar, a British naval base on the northwest tip of Bermuda, to question the surviving crew members. In the dazzling summer sunlight the *Zawisza Czarny*'s captain, Jan Sauer, kneeled to write "M-A-R-Q-U-E-S" in red chalk on the concrete platform, one hundred yards from the sea. Behind the Polish captain stood the survivors—barefoot, sunburned boys with haggard eyes and toes scarred by the rigging.

Under "M-A-R-Q-U-E-S," Captain Sauer printed "C-H-R-I-S-T-O-P-H-E-R" in yellow chalk. Little Christopher, the fifteen-month-old son of *Marques* Captain Stuart Finlay, was the youngest believed dead of the sixty-seven-year-old tall ship. A Polish crewman laid a bouquet of red carnations and baby's breath on this heartfelt memorial, the first of many services to be held during the next few weeks for the nineteen who were lost.

After a moment of silence the press conference began. Captain Sauer's stiff account of the rescue of eight of the *Marques*'s crew Sunday morning was translated from Polish into monosyllabic English by a female interpreter from his crew. As Sauer's account dragged on, Bobby Cooper left his chair and sat on the edge of the platform, his back to the press, smoking a cigarette and gazing tensely out to sea where the search continued for his ship and his "family," who were either struggling for life in the choppy seas or buried 800 feet below.

Then reporters unleashed a series of rapid questions intimating carelessness on the part of the crew or neglect in the maintenance of the ship. "Why didn't the *Marques* have a hydraulic release system at the helm?" one reporter asked.

"Because she was a floating antique," Bill Barnhardt curtly reminded him.

"I love the sea," Cooper told the cameras and tape recorders without looking at the journalists, one of whom had stepped forward onto the flowers to get a better picture. "I'm very lucky. I'm very upset."

At dusk Wednesday the Coast Guard officially called off the search for those still missing from the *Marques*. Searchers had crisscrossed 3,600 square miles of ocean under good conditions with sophisticated heat-sensing equipment and found no one. Despite water temperatures above 70 degrees, it was believed that only the eight rescued by the *Zawisza Czarny,* and Stu Gillespie, en route to Halifax aboard the *Assinboine,* had been saved.

August, 1984

⚓

FASTEST EVER

We drive the new, world-record-setting, forty-seven-foot Fountain power catamaran to 162 miles per hour.

BY PETER A. JANSSEN

As I gripped the wheel, trying to keep the forty-seven-foot, 2,400-horsepower catamaran under control as we absolutely screamed up North Carolina's Pamlico River, I could hear Fabio Buzzi, eight-time world raceboat champion who was sitting behind me as throttleman, counting off our speed over the headset attached to my helmet. "145 . . . 150 . . . 152 . . ."

There was very little, if anything, of the boat—a big red sled—actually in the water. The idea of keeping it under control was theoretical, at best. About an hour before, Reggie Fountain, the boat's builder, had driven the boat, sitting where I was sitting now, and, with Fabio throttling, had set a new world record of 158.31 miles per hour through a one-kilometer course. After he returned to the dock he asked if I'd like to give it a try. Sure, I said. Be careful, Reggie warned. "It's like skating on ice."

Except that the ice kept shifting. "155," Fabio counted

behind me. To say that I was terrified (155 miles an hour does require your total concentration) would be an understatement. As we had climbed into the boat, Fabio had reminded me that three offshore cats like this one (except slower) had turned over in races last season. And Fabio's usual racing partner had lost an arm in a crash.

We were going upwind and even though it was barely registering at 5 knots or so, puffs started to nudge the starboard sponson; the wind hit again and the boat was right on the edge.

"We're losing it, Fabio," I reported into the headset mike, keeping my voice as calm and businesslike as I possibly could. "Okay," he replied, in his reassuring, professional, and cultured voice. Buzzi, fifty-four, is a native Italian; he speaks English fluently but with enough of a European accent to make him sound something like a combination of Marcello Mastroianni and your favorite doctor. Fabio dialed back on the throttles and we swept into a wide turn, very wide, since the boat, with Buzzi's Trimax surface drives turning 33-inch props, was made for running in a straight line, not a slalom course.

Wide as it was, the turn was high-speed in order to stay on plane. Everything is relative, of course, so we turned at about 60 to 70 miles per hour. The boat comes up on plane at 50 miles per hour.

Now, we headed downriver again. On our first run, we stayed in the low 150s. But this time I felt more confident; I know that Fabio was more confident in me. The water was flat; the temperature cold, very cold.

Coming out of the turn, I could see the stake boats out along what had been the kilo course; now, since we were not running for an official record, they were more spread out, covering a mile or so. Considering the hazards involved, each boat had a diver and a paramedic. Another diver was on the helicopter overhead with photographer Roy Attaway, although its top speed was about 100. (I figured if we turned over it would catch up with us pretty quickly.) As I straightened us out and Fabio hit the throttles, I mentally went through his precautions one more time. Back at the dock, as I was putting on my helmet, he had looked me directly in the eye and imparted his instructions.

"First," he said, "if we turn over, don't panic." (I tried to imagine myself upside down in a forty-seven-foot cat and, if I wasn't dead or severely injured, remembering not to panic.)

Second, "reach for your air," Fabio said. An emergency oxygen bottle was strapped into the cockpit immediately next to my right leg, with the mouthpiece held on top by a rubber band. The bottle was turned on, so (if the boat turned over and I didn't panic) all I had to do was put the mouthpiece in my mouth so I could breathe. Third, I was to wait until the cockpit filled almost all the way up (or down, since we were upside down) with water and then I should release my safety harness. This was a large web harness coming over each shoulder, with another strap coming up through the seat between my legs; the entire affair came together in a big buckle in my lap.

Finally, Fabio said, I should reach over my left shoulder and open the overhead hatch in the canopy (it had a large, easy-to-grasp stainless steel lever) and then pull myself out of the cockpit (which, needless to say, is upside down underwater).

Fabio had my entire, riveted attention as he told me all

this, but once we were in the boat he had me repeat the
sequence, actually putting the mouthpiece in my mouth,
undoing the safety harness, opening the hatch, telling him
that I would remember not to panic. In fact, I was very
grateful for this advice, and for Fabio's manner. An accident at speeds over 100 miles per hour could easily be
fatal; it was reassuring, and somehow quite calming, to
be prepared.

As we headed down the course Fabio started reading
off the speed again. In seconds, it seemed, he calmly
stated, "90 . . . 100 . . . 110 . . . turbo." (The turbochargers
kick in at 110 miles per hour and they give you the kind
of boost that you'd expect in a fighter jet; you go from
110 to 130 in a big hurry.)

Now we were beginning to get that skating-on-ice feeling again, when any tiny change could bring on instanta-
neous disaster. As we simply flew past the shoreline, I
gripped the black Momo wheel and made just the slightest
adjustments to correct our course. The biggest immediate
decision was how to pass the stake boats. We were going
so fast that any decision like this was basic instinct; we
were already past them before I had time to really think
about it.

As we screamed down river in the big red cat, kicking
up an enormous rooster tail, Fabio's voice got more excited. "145 . . . 150 . . . 155 . . ."

I made a slight correction for more open water, a long
stretch of open water. The stake boats now were well
behind us; the helicopter, history. We were on our own
and we were flying. Right on the edge. But, at least I
thought I knew where the edge was.

As the boat skittered, I glanced at the oxygen bottle
rubbing against my right leg. *No time for that*, I thought.

Concentrate, concentrate. If I concentrate hard enough, I thought, *everything will be all right.* (There really wasn't any choice. The hatch overhead was so tight that, wearing my racing helmet and vest, it would have been almost impossible to get out even in the best of circumstances.)

Concentration, I thought, *meant survival.*

"160," Fabio said, his voice rising. "162," he said, his voice breaking with excitement. "162 . . . 162. . . ." *Hang on,* I told myself, *hang on. No mistakes now.* I was nudging the wheel out of sheer instinct. We flew, skittered, screamed down the river. Absolutely at the edge of the envelope. All alone, totally alone. The barren February low country shoreline only accentuated the sense of isolation. It was the greatest adrenaline rush you can possibly imagine.

After a while Fabio dialed back until we once again swept through a wide right-hand turn for another pass up the river. I looked up and found the helicopter a long way away, bearing down on us. The chase boats were mere specks in the distance.

Now it seemed almost routine: "90 . . . 100 . . . 110 . . . turbo." Feel the jolt as the turbos kick in and the boat hurtles ahead. We screamed under the helicopter coming down to meet us as Fabio edged the throttles up to the low 150s; we were past the stake boats before I even worried about them. This time, although we were pushing the razor-thin borderline of control, we kept going. We were skating on ice, but even with the wind nudging the starboard bow I didn't need to tell Fabio that we were losing it.

The end of the run. Time to head in. A crowd of people tied up the boat and helped us get out. Fabio told them we'd hit 162 and said, "It's the fastest I've ever gone." In fact, it's the fastest anyone has ever gone in that type of boat.

Then, ever the gentleman, he turned to me and said, smiling, "I enjoyed riding with you."

May, 1997

⚓

ADRIFT IN THE SOUTH PACIFIC

After their sailboat is sunk, a family must survive for twenty-four days in a dinghy and an inflatable life raft.

BY SHEARLEAN DUKE

It had been an idyllic first year of cruising for Margaret and Robert Aros and Robert's seventeen-year-old son Christian. And it was a warm, calm November night in the South Pacific as a fresh westerly wind pushed *Vamonos*, their thirty-six-foot Lapworth sloop, toward New Zealand.

Then, around midnight, just three days out of Raratonga, the peaceful world aboard *Vamonos* came to a sudden end. Robert Aros, lying asleep in his bunk while Margaret stood watch, remembers being jostled awake. Christian remembers hearing an ominous thud, and then the hiss of water. Margaret, the only one to actually see what happened, felt a terrifying crash, and heard a *"Boom, Boom."* The next thing she knew the boat was lying on its port side and water was gurgling through *Vamonos*'s slender, and once-sturdy, mahogany hull.

During the next thirty minutes, *Vamonos*, which had

carried the Aros family—Robert, fifty, Margaret, thirty, and her stepson Christian—safely over 5,000 miles of ocean from California to Mexico and on into the South Pacific, was violently ripped open and disappeared into the ocean as four- to five-foot waves pounded the boat and swept it across a treacherous reef. The Aros family never saw the reef—but they will never forget it either.

Abandoning ship on November 9 with what little they could salvage and load into their eight-foot dinghy and an eight-foot inflatable, the family set off on a hellish twenty-four-day voyage that took them 1,200 miles to a tiny sand bar near the Fiji Islands. There, with Robert just days away from death, the three were finally rescued.

The story of Robert, Margaret, and Christian Aros is a story of courage, determination, undying religious faith, and tremendous luck: both good and bad. "They told us it was a million-to-one chance that we hit that reef," said Margaret, safe again in the family's Long Beach home. But it was also a million-to-one chance that the starving trio would be rescued once they landed on a seldom-visited sand bar in the Lau Island group, where they were picked up by some local fishermen on December 5.

Robert Aros had been involved in boating since 1952 when he built his first vessel, a twelve-foot runabout. He was an experienced sailor who'd begun planning and preparing for his two-year dream voyage six years before. An articulate, candid man, Aros, still thin but not emaciated, sat at home in front of a roaring fireplace, and recalled those final thirty minutes when, due to a navigational error, *Vamonos* crashed into the submerged reef and the family prepared to abandon ship.

"It was 11:30 in the evening and Chris and I were asleep. Margaret was on watch. I was tossed around in my berth and jumped up and saw that we were on a reef. We were lying there on our port side. We must have jumped up on the reef and the water was about two feet deep. It was a flat plateau, very smooth. So we must have hit it and bounced onto it. We were traveling along at about 7 knots, really moving on a port tack. By rights, we should have landed on our starboard side."

Landing on the port side was an unlucky break, as Margaret soon discovered. "I went below to send an SOS," she said. But the ICOM 720 ham radio, which was mounted just below the companionway on the port side, was partially submerged and inoperable. They did not have an EPIRB radio beacon onboard.

"The last thing Bob wanted to do was abandon *Vamonos*," said Margaret. "Bob always instructed us to stay with the ship. He always said, 'Do not abandon ship unless your ship is gone.' When we stepped off the *Vamonos* into the dinghy the boom was nearly under water."

In fact, during the first twenty minutes after the accident, Chris, one of Robert's five children from a former marriage, and his dad worked frantically trying to secure the boat to the reef, in an effort to save it.

"We lost about twenty minutes trying to secure the boat," Robert said, "but it was obvious that the boat was going to go over the edge of the reef and back into the ocean. I could see the cabin lights shining through the bottom of the boat. There were no big holes in the boat, but the planking had separated and you could see light maybe a quarter of an inch."

"By the time we were ready to leave the boat, water was up to my waist," recalled Christian, who had been sailing since he was ten.

"The last trip I made down into the cabin for supplies,

the water was to my waist, too," Margaret said. "I was afraid to go below again because I was afraid I would be swept away with the boat."

Once it was obvious that *Vamonos* was beyond saving, the Aroses had only five or six minutes to actually abandon ship. During that time Christian, who says, "We were scared out of our minds," managed to pump up the Avon inflatable in what he estimated to be no more than sixty seconds. Margaret, who had been filling a pillowcase with whatever food she could manage to find in the shambles below, worked as fast as possible to grab what she could. She managed to get the sextant and the sight reduction tables, but she did not salvage the nautical almanac Robert needed to use the sextant.

When Margaret looked around to take stock of the family's meager supplies once they were in the dinghy, she found: A Jehovah's Witness yearbook for 1981 (which proved to be invaluable to the devoutly religious family); a first-aid kit; a duffle bag full of Christian's clothes; some fishing equipment (with which they never caught a fish); a few flares; three dinners of dried food; seventeen cans of fruits and vegetables (only the vegetable locker had been accessible); five gallons of gasoline-tainted water in a jerry can; ten bags of salted peanuts; a solar still (which never worked); an oar; a can opener; a couple of knives; several needles; a sheet off one of the sails; some nylon rope; Margaret's glasses; and a chart of the Tonga area.

While Margaret was taking stock, Robert was busy grabbing Christian's twelve-foot Cyclone sailboard, which was strapped to *Vamonos*'s liferail and easily accessible. "I got the mast, the sail and the board, but not the skegs," he recalled. The sailboard proved to be one of the most useful items salvaged.

Although Christian had lots of clothes because of the lucky duffle bag, Robert Aros, who was nude when the crash occurred, had only the Farmer John wetsuit he quickly donned during those first hectic moments. The wetsuit chafed his infected skin so badly he had to wear Christian's clothes, which Margaret ripped apart and then painstakingly resewed, using strands of nylon unraveled from the salvaged rope.

After *Vamonos* sank, the Aroses had an eight-foot Sandpiper dinghy and the eight-foot Avon Redcrest inflatable. Robert managed to rig the windsurfer sail on the Sandpiper and, using an oar to steer, guided his tiny convoy through heavy following seas. "I tied the two boats stern to stern so that we would have a pointed front end and a pointed back end to break the following seas," he explained. "We carried most of our supplies in the soft dinghy, towing the windsurfer—an excellent sea anchor." But the inflatable was capsized at least a dozen times by twenty to thirty foot waves. Each time the boat went over, another precious item of food, clothing, or medicine was lost to the sea.

Because the inflatable had been punctured and patched, it had to be pumped up every day. When, after nearly twenty days at sea, even the pump was washed overboard, Margaret and Christian took turns blowing the dinghy up by mouth. By then Robert was too weak to help.

By the end of the first week, all three survivors were covered by painful open sores and staph infections caused by the constant exposure to salt water. "I never thought about drowning or sharks," Margaret said. "Drowning at some point wouldn't have hurt so bad. We were in so much pain. Drowning was just another death."

The family's starvation diet for nineteen days included

one can of vegetables each morning, split three ways. In the beginning there were also the peanuts, which they usually ate in the afternoon.

"I started rationing the food right away," Robert said. "And I was in charge of it. Each morning I would crawl into the hard boat and open the can and we'd pass it around. Our favorite was fruit cocktail. We had two of those. And we had one of peaches. The rest were of corn and green beans. The worst was the artichoke hearts. That was terrible. They were so cold and stringy. We had no idea what was in each can because there were no labels."

After nineteen days, when all the food was gone, including the dried meals, they went for two days with no food at all.

Then there was the incident with the booby bird.

"Boobies are strange," Robert said. "They will just fly up and look right at you. This one landed on the bow."

"Chris yelled at me to grab it," Margaret said. "So I grabbed him by the feet."

"He bit Margaret and then he bit me," Robert added.

Once the bird was caught, there was still a problem of how to kill it because of the Aros' strict religious beliefs.

"We did have a problem of killing it because we are Jehovah's Witnesses. In our religion you have to kill it properly and by then we had lost all our knives. We couldn't strangle him because that would be against our religion," Robert said.

They finally devised an approved method of slaughter, using one of Margaret's needles and a piece of the fishing line.

"We took the needle and put it through his neck," Robert said. "And then we used the line and cut his neck open and bled him," since drinking the blood would have also been against their religion.

That day they had raw booby meat from the five-pound bird. "We hung the rest up on the mast and the next day had duck jerky," joked Robert.

They used the inedible parts for bait, but still had no luck fishing.

As the twenty-second day dawned, the trio was badly dehydrated. They had only a little rain which supplied just about a liter of water, Margaret said.

Robert had begun to hallucinate. "We were progressively going downhill," he said. "Oh, I remember everything. Even when I was hallucinating. I remember my hallucinations about having four people in the boat."

During the entire twenty-four days afloat, Robert says they never saw another boat, an airplane, a shark, or a whale. The only fish they saw were five tiny flying fish which landed in the dinghy and which they promptly devoured.

Every day they prayed that they would either find an island or that rescuers would find them.

The lowest point came when the inflatable dinghy overturned and the last of the precious water supply began to drift away. "We were all in the water at first and grabbing everything we could," Christian said. "The water started floating away and Margaret went after it. Dad and I got in the dinghy and I saw Margaret was floating away. The wind had already begun to push the dinghy at a pretty rapid speed away from her. So I got on the windsurfer and took the oar and started paddling toward her. By the time I got to her, we were probably 40 yards from the dinghy. Then we started paddling toward Dad, but we couldn't keep up with his speed. I was shouting to him but he couldn't hear me."

"Half the time I couldn't even see them," Robert said. "It was frightening and the things that passed through my mind were that they are going to be lost and we will not see each other again. Will I be alone in this dinghy? Will they be alone out there? It seemed to take forever, but actually all this happened in five or ten minutes."

"Margaret was lying on the front of the board and crying," Christian said. "I said, 'Margaret, Margaret, we've got to keep going. We aren't going to die out here.' So then she'd paddle some more. Finally I told her to look up. We were almost there. Then she started to paddle her daylights out.

"When we finally got back to the dinghy we just got off the sailboard and all crawled into the boat, which was full of water and we huddled together and cried and held each other."

On the twenty-fourth day Margaret spotted land. "We couldn't believe it," she said.

"We directed ourselves toward it and by midafternoon we were five miles from it," Robert said. "Then the current started to take us away from it. By then there were five islands in sight and it didn't look like we could make any of them. So I took the sail down. Then we saw the sand bar coming up and we realized the current was taking us away from that, too!

"But we could see the bottom so Chris jumped over and tied the boat to the coral. We stayed there like that for three or four hours until the current and wind subsided and we felt we had a good chance to make it. Margaret jumped overboard and untied the rope while Chris and I paddled. We made it."

By then Robert was so weak he could not stand up.

Fortunately, they found some bird's eggs on the sandbar and ate them. Margaret also found three or four coconuts which had been washed ashore.

"There were no trees on this sandbar," she said. "The coconuts had drifted from other islands and had already started to sprout. And this is a very important point," she said. "Probably nobody would have even hassled with a coconut like that, but I soaked them and it was kind of like the old telephone book trick. You know, you can tear a telephone book in half if you tear it page by page. So I started shredding fibers off the husk and when I got it completely husked we broke it. Inside was a soft, white, sponge-like ball. We shared that. That's what we ate."

But after two days on the sandbar, Robert says, "We realized that this was just another death. It was as much as death as the sea was. So we were going to leave that afternoon and try to make one of the islands about twelve miles away. But before noon this boat came up. Margaret spotted it first. By that time I couldn't walk or even stand up. Chris and Margaret waved their jackets so they would spot us. We almost couldn't believe it, we were so elated. We were thanking God over and over again."

The rescuers were a group of fishermen led by Leonard Tolhurst, a teacher at Fulton College in Fiji, who had come to the sandbar to go shelling and to check some banded birds. The shipwrecked family found out later that the sandbar is usually visited only once a year.

By then the Aroses were so weak that Margaret remembers having to be carried to the bathroom at the tiny village where their rescuers first took them. Doctors in Suva said that Robert was perhaps two days away from death. Normally thin at 155 pounds, Robert weighed 115 pounds when he was rescued. Margaret, who started out at 140 pounds, weighed only 100 pounds. Christian, normally 125 pounds, also weighed only 100. The family spent three weeks recuperating in Suva before returning home to Long Beach.

Do they plan to go cruising again?

"When we got to the hospital and survived this thing," Robert said, "we didn't want to ever be in the water again. I still feel that way. I won't even go swimming in salt water; in fresh water, yes, but salt water, no. We were so miserable and uncomfortable and in so much pain from the sores. But time has a way of changing things. And the cruising life, that's something else. That day-to-day life was so wonderful. I've been under so much pressure since I've been back, that I've had many sleepless nights. Just in driving the freeway last night the thought occurred to me: This is a lousy life compared to cruising."

April, 1983

⚓

SUNRIDER

Environmentalist Bryan Peterson drives a twenty-four-foot Zodiac around the world—powered by soybean oil and solar energy.

BY POLLY WHITTELL

Some people have to check the *Guinness Book of World Records* to find out if they've really accomplished a historic feat. Not so for forty-nine-year-old Bryan Peterson who, against all odds, recently drove his twenty-four-foot Zodiac *Sunrider* triumphantly under San Francisco's Golden Gate Bridge to complete a two-year, 35,000-mile voyage around the world—a voyage so unique there's hardly competition. Peterson is undoubtedly the first person ever to circumnavigate the world in an inflatable boat—with a stock 180-horsepower MerCruiser diesel stern drive fueled by soybean oil, no less. *Sunrider* is also reportedly the smallest powerboat ever to complete a circumnavigation.

But Peterson's goal wasn't to get into the record books at all. The purpose of the Sunrider Expedition, using the Zodiac as a floating ecological classroom, was to demonstrate to the world the viability of an environmentally friendly, renewable fuel—in this case soydiesel, a form of Biodiesel made of soybean oil, as an alternative to petroleum diesel—and to show the efficiency of solar energy in powering the boat's electronics.

Peterson's eclectic, adventuresome career seemed to uniquely suit him to the Sunrider Expedition. After an early fling with the Southern California surfing life, he lived in Hawaii for a time, then settled in Fairfield, Iowa, his present hometown. Along the way he did stints as an Air Force corpsman, policeman, firefighter, tour-boat operator, actor, rock-concert organizer, venture capitalist, and publisher of travel and environmental guides for *USA Today*—one of the inspirations for the expedition. Another was his twenty years as a paramedic in emergency care and rescue work—often carried out in Zodiacs.

Sunrider was a twenty-four-foot Zodiac Hurricane 730 Rescue/Patrol boat with a rigid, modified-deep-V hull and inflatable buoyancy collar, provided by Zodiac Hurricane Marine of Richmond, British Columbia. It had a watertight aluminum cuddy cabin custom-built by Adrenalin Marine in North Vancouver, British Columbia. Solar panels on the aluminum canopy would generate about 160 watts of electricity in good weather, and together with the MerCruiser's alternator, feed the batteries that powered the boat's roughly $100,000 worth of state-of-the-art electronics—which included a Cetrek/Wagner autopilot, Garmin GPS, Raytheon radar, Furuno loran and depthsounder, a chart plotter, a COMSAT satellite-based computer communications system, and SSB and VHF radios. The Zodiac's MerCruiser diesel stern drive was backed up by a 27-horsepower Yanmar diesel outboard for emergencies.

Sunrider's four permanent below-decks fuel tanks held 280 gallons of soydiesel, and flexible bladder tanks and portable drums could carry another 500-plus above-deck. But on the first long Pacific leg from the West Coast to Honolulu, Hawaii, Peterson arranged to have an oceangoing tug, the *Chinook*, serve as a floating filling station en route.

The voyage got off to an inauspicious start when, just north of San Francisco, en route to Oregon to rendezvous with the tug, Peterson and his twelve-year-old son Danny, who was planning to accompany him at least as far as Hawaii, hit a gale with winds gusting to 40 knots and breaking seas of up to sixteen feet. "It was kind of like going down Pike's Peak without brakes and not being able to see," Peterson says. "But *Sunrider* did just what it was supposed to do; I was never worried." Danny, on the other hand, *was*—and headed straight back home to Iowa.

Due to a series of delays, *Sunrider*'s departure from Oregon got pushed into the height of the Pacific's fall hurricane season, but Peterson managed to make it to Hawaii during a relative calm between two storms. "The crossing was really a cruise, a real pleasure," he says. "Everything worked perfectly." And though he managed only about four to five hours of sleep every twenty-four hours, mostly in catnaps while on autopilot, he did find time to practice his transcendental meditation for relaxation.

Peterson was able to gear *Sunrider*'s speed to the tugboat's—about 7 or 8 knots—most of the way. While the tug was often out of sight, he generally tried to stay within a few miles of it in order to refuel every couple of days. After five refuelings, he went on ahead for the last 200 miles, increasing his speed to about 20 to 24 knots. With a lighter load and an alternate prop, the Zodiac can plane at speeds up to 30 knots.

Sunrider covered the 2,200-mile leg to Hawaii in 12 days, using about 800 gallons of fuel. At speeds of 7 to 9 knots, the boat gets roughly 2 to 4 miles per gallon, Peterson says. "Soydiesel offers virtually the same performance and consumption as petroleum diesel," he says, "without modification or harm to the engine, and with tremendous environmental benefits."

For boaters, one of these is that when soydiesel burns, instead of the usual noxious petroleum diesel fumes, the appetizing aroma of Chinese cooking wafts across the deck. But more important are the facts that it's renewable, as well as biodegradable, nonpolluting and nontoxic when it spills (in fact, Peterson even rubbed it onto his skin as suntan oil when he got too much on his hands). Plus, it's much cleaner-burning than petroleum diesel, emitting 70 percent less smoke, significantly less nitrous oxide, and 100 percent less sulfur (which contributes to acid rain).

Sunrider's smooth passage to Hawaii seemed to bode well for the voyage. But the moment Peterson set off for the South Pacific, barely fifty miles out of Honolulu, the stern drive suddenly conked out and the boat had to be towed back in by the Coast Guard. The problem: *chocolate* mixed in with the soy sauce! It seemed the last fuel drums hadn't had their previous contents thoroughly washed out.

So, after further delays for repairs, Peterson started off again in the spring, this time accompanied by Danny. The boy proved to be an indispensable hand on the long Pacific crossing from Hawaii to Australia. Since *Sunrider*'s alternator hadn't yet been hooked up properly, the batteries that ran the electronics could only be charged from the solar cells—on clear days. So there were long stretches where Peterson, without enough juice for his autopilot, would have to hand-steer all night and rely on Danny to fill in during the day while he took catnaps.

During the 1,200-mile leg to Christmas Island near the Equator and the subsequent 1,300-mile stretch to American and Western Samoa, the seas kept building till they reached fifteen to twenty-five feet—three times as tall as the boat. "Sometimes they would shoot us straight up in the air," says Peterson, "or crash into the boat's side or over the top."

From the Samoas to Fiji, the big challenge was threading the Nanuku Passage—200 miles of waters full of reefs, uncharted islands and shipwrecks. Then, on finally reaching Suva, Fiji, relief turned to consternation when Peterson learned his soydiesel shipment had mysteriously disappeared: Seems it had accidentally been sold to some local restaurants as salad oil! It took some fancy explaining to get it back. But the incident didn't detract from the place. "The scenery was incredible, and the Fijians are the most friendly, nice, innocent, beautiful people anywhere," Peterson says.

Another favorite was the next stop, Vanuatu, a group of archetypal South Pacific islands that Peterson says is "a place I could move to and live in the rest of my life. In fact, there's just one island after another like that. Those dream places are all there, all perfect—hundreds of little islands that look like postcards, that you could live on; hundreds of Hawaiis, but with no one on them, or with tribes who've never had contact with civilization. If you're looking for bare-breasted natives in grass skirts and grass huts, they're *everywhere* in the South Pacific, everywhere *except* the places you always hear about."

Then came exotic Papua New Guinea, Southeast Asia, "where warring tribes are still killing each other with spears and bones," says Peterson. "Men can have as many wives as they want, and the going price for a wife is twenty pigs. Part of a wife's duty is to pre-chew food for the piglets."

It was off New Guinea that Peterson had two of his hairiest experiences. One night in a narrow Louisiade Archipelago channel he almost got sandwiched between two huge ships crossing paths. "It was scary—we barely got out of the way in time," he says, as the little Zodiac tended not to show up on ships' radars. On another night in the treacherous Torres Strait between New Guinea and Australia, where a fast current squeezes through the narrow passage among hundreds of islands, reefs, and ships, *Sunrider*'s stern drive suddenly quit when some debris blocked the fuel line, while at the same time its GPS temporarily went out. Peterson squeaked through by switching to the outboard and using dead reckoning.

Coming into Australia's Thursday Islands one night soon afterward was an adventure, too, when *Sunrider* was met by a fishing boat "full of armed men wearing fatigues, with their faces painted black," Peterson says. "We'd been warned that there are pirates in this area." Though they turned out to be friendly Aussie commandos on a military exercise, the Zodiac was accosted shortly thereafter and sent packing by some *not*-so-friendly Aussies—a band of crocodiles.

Danny flew home from Darwin, Australia, where Peterson met a Brazilian sailor and video producer, Wilfredo Schurmann, who agreed to carry some extra fuel for *Sunrider* aboard his fifty-five-foot sloop *Guapos* on the long Indian Ocean crossing. That helped Peterson get to the next stop, another Christmas Island about 1,800 miles to the west, where he arrived in time for "one of the most amazing sights I've ever seen—a seasonal migration of 120 million crabs laying their eggs. They cover the streets and march right through the houses."

From here to the mid-ocean islands of Cocos of Diego Garcia, a U.S. naval base, Peterson battled some of the roughest seas of his voyage. For more than 2,000 miles during almost two weeks he had strong winds and huge following swells of fifteen to thirty feet. "We'd scream over these monstrous waves," he says. "It was like going over one waterfall after another. But I picked the right boat. Other boats yaw coming down the faces of waves, but this one keeps going straight. Imagine surfing down a wave at 30 knots—sometimes on autopilot, and not burying the nose once. I was never even thrown out of my seat"—though now and then a rogue wave would suddenly spin the boat around. But by the time he reached port, the stress of the big seas had caused the gearboxes on both engines to blow, so *Sunrider* had to be towed in for repairs.

On the next 1,200-mile leg to the Seychelle Islands, the stern drive's oil cooler went out, too, so Peterson had to go most of the way using his little backup outboard. But Mahé in the Seychelles was worth the slow trip. "With its combination of rocks and lush tropical vegetation, it's one of the most breathtaking islands I have ever seen," he says.

The northern Indian Ocean's impending monsoon season plus the unrest in Somalia now made Peterson's planned Red Sea route unsafe, so he changed course and began heading southwest toward Madagascar—and less obvious dangers. One night *Sunrider* suddenly hit what was probably a big log washed down from the rain forest, which sent the boat out of control and busted a prop. At sunup, Peterson, tethered to the stern, dove overboard to replace the prop, becoming submerged whenever a swell would roll by—while his buddy on *Guapos* circled the Zodiac to keep the local shark population at bay. Another close call came a few days later when, just five feet from the Zodiac, "a huge shark bigger than the boat suddenly leapt out of the water and made a fast meal of a dead penguin floating by," says Peterson, who held on tight. "I didn't want to be dessert."

At the island of Nose Be, Madagascar, Peterson found "the underwater sea life so thick it looks like you could walk on it, and so many seabirds they clog the radar." He took in quite a show—a gliding manta ray bigger than the boat, a giant leaping porpoise, breaching whales, an island populated by monkeylike lemurs, outrigger canoes filled with bananas, prows with old sheets for sails. "Madagascar is the most interesting, exotic, stimulating, absolutely mind-boggling place I've ever been," he says. The town of Hellville, a onetime French colonial settlement now in ruins and overgrown with foliage, "looks like a set for a Humphrey Bogart movie. It's a magical place," he says, with its eclectic mix of peoples, religions, and ideologies.

Peterson now began harbor-hopping his way down the coast of South Africa toward Cape Town. In Richards Bay, he spent the night in the local jail, "just to catch up on some sleep." Arriving in Durban at a peak time of turmoil, he was accosted by a patrol boat filled with huge Afrikaner policemen—who wound up inviting him to play volleyball. "This place is wild," he says. At that time there were dozens of daily shootings and bombings, including a bomb that exploded less than 100 yards from the boat.

Back out at sea, things got pretty wild, too. As *Sunrider* proceeded around Africa's treacherous Cape of Good Hope to Cape Town, it was blasted by a sudden storm packing hurricane-force winds of 65 knots gusting to 90, with twenty-foot breaking seas topped by six to eight feet of whitewater and spindrift. "The waves would crash over the boat and shoot under the canopy, drenching me, while the spindrift reduced my visibility to zero," says Peterson. The battering continued for seven hours, with nowhere to hide. "This was the first time on the voyage that I felt real fear and wondered if I was going to make it," he says. "But the Zodiac handled the storm beautifully—it just pops up like a cork." By the time *Sunrider* was able to limp into the Royal Cape Yacht Club, there had been a good deal of equipment damage, however, including the loss of both steering and communications.

After repairs were made, an undaunted Peterson headed up the Atlantic coast of Africa in fifteen- to twenty-foot seas to Namibia, escorted for a while by groups of seals and dolphins competing with each other "as if in a circus act, doing tandem spirals and back flips." Equally dramatic was the coastline itself, where the forty-story-high dunes of the Kalahari Desert reach right to the sea, and the beaches and seabeds are studded with diamonds. "But," says Peterson, "there are posted warnings not to approach the coast or you'll be shot." He passed fleets of diamond-mining boats carrying divers and dredges that suck up the gems. One boat was rumored to have made over $20 million in less than an hour, he says.

While heading northwest from Walvis Bay, Namibia, to St. Helena, 1,200 miles offshore, *Sunrider* suddenly lost its steering, and Peterson had to bleed the system at sea. On arriving at the island—the place where Napoleon was exiled and now the site of a small British-style fishing village—a tremendous surge and five-foot breaking seas made it necessary to go ashore by water taxi. "They bring you to a big rock when the water is rising," says Peterson. "Then you grab hold of a rope, jump onto the rock, and the rope swings you ashore before the water again drops six feet. Even little old ladies do it."

After his next stop at Ascension Island 800 miles to the northwest, Peterson embarked on a 1,600-mile passage to Recife, Brazil, joined along the way by "more than 200 porpoises, as far as the eye could see." Then one morning he awoke to the shock of finding half of *Sunrider's* port side collapsed—with a foot-long gash in one of the ten-foot tubes, which had been hit during the night. Amazingly, he says, "the boat's performance wasn't affected."

In Recife, Peterson had a visit from his wife, Janice, and while waiting for *Sunrider* to be hauled for repairs—which took six weeks—they enjoyed a tour of Rio de Janeiro and São Paulo. Once the boat was ready and Janice had left, Peterson proceeded on up the coast. At one point about fifty miles offshore, he encountered a strange phenomenon—a wide ribbon of white, muddy water that looked like a sandbar, though the depthsounder showed good depth. During the next twenty-four hours as *Sunrider* fought its way northwest across the line, the boat kept spinning around in different directions, "as if it was on ice," he says. The cause turned out to be the outflow from the mighty Amazon, the world's largest river.

A desire to explore the rain forest led Peterson up a smaller river at Cayenne, French Guiana, to an anchorage at a narrow point "where the forest started closing in, and I spent the night listening to the wild jungle sounds." He put in again for some minor repairs up the coast at the Dutch town of Paramaribo, Suriname, then got refueled at Port of Spain, Trinidad, where he found excellent boating facilities. En route to Venezuela, the engine quit due to a leak in the cooling-system hose, so Peterson put in at the huge Naiquata Yacht Club in Caracas while the local Mercury dealer replaced it (more expedient than waiting for repairs).

Danny rejoined Peterson on the Dutch resort island of Aruba off Venezuela, and *Sunrider* departed for the Panama Canal. Peterson had been warned to give Colombia a wide berth because of the prevalence of pirates. But at one point about fifty miles off the Colombian coast, as the heavily laden Zodiac was slowly making its way west, Peterson suddenly spotted a forty-foot boat about a mile away that kept closing till it was only twenty feet off. Five swarthy, glaring men began waving their shirts indicating they wanted to come alongside. Peterson warned them off by radio, changed direction and started running, but they continued their pursuit. After sending a sat com message (he'd been without the SSB since the storm at Cape Town) to his project manager, Martin Del Re, in Seattle, asking that the Coast Guard be alerted, Peterson attempted to intimidate the men by waving a machete and videotaping them. Then Danny popped up out of the hatch pointing a filler tube that resembled a rifle barrel— and the men finally fell off. "I'm not sure what deterred them, but it was really scary," says Peterson.

This was also one of the roughest legs of the trip, he says. The worst moment came one night around midnight as *Sunrider* was running in ten- to fifteen-foot seas. He was at the helm, with Danny asleep on top of the engine cover, when, all of a sudden, says Peterson, "out of nowhere, a rogue wave—a wall of water as high as the boat—crashed into the port side, blew out the side curtain, filled the cockpit, and put Danny completely under. He awoke sputtering with a mouthful of water—I thought he was really choking.''

But then *Sunrider*'s transit of the Panama Canal was a cakewalk, taking just eight hours. ''We ran on plane, dodging crocodiles, through the small-boat shortcut,'' says Peterson. ''My first view of the Pacific Ocean was really a thrill. I consider it *my* ocean—my home waters.''

Heading northwest to Golfito, Costa Rica, *Sunrider* was buzzed by some men in a military plane ''who seemed to think we were a drug boat,'' says Peterson. In Golfito, everyone warned them about ''Rambo,'' the stern customs officer who insists all paperwork must be letter-perfect. But the resulting delays gave them a chance to visit an ecological retreat. ''Costa Rica is just beautiful,'' says Peterson. ''If you sit in one place in the rain forest, there is so much diversity that you see something new each minute—exotic birds, screeching howler monkeys, picture-perfect waterfalls, and monkey ladders—twisted vines that you'd expect to see Tarzan swinging from.''

After a brief stop at the Puerto Quetzal, Guatemala, naval base, the big priority now was to move northward quickly, as they were in the midst of the Pacific Coast hurricane season. Soon after entering Mexico's Gulf of Tehuantepec, where most of the storms are spawned, *Sunrider* was suddenly hit by 60- to 70-knot winds and seas over fifteen feet, pushing them dangerously close to the lee shore. ''The whole sky was electric,'' says Peterson. ''I had to turn off most of the electronics. We were continually blinded by lightning all around us for a full hour. I expected to be hit. It was terrifying, really wild—the wildest weather I'd seen since the storm at Cape Town.''

The next morning, off the coast of Mexico, *Sunrider*'s universal engine/drive joint gave way, having long outlasted its normal lifetime. So Peterson put into the Mexican naval base at Puerto Madero, the main port of Chiapas, where he found the Zapatista rebellion in full swing. Before they knew it, *Sunrider* was surrounded and rammed, its hull dented, by two launches full of yelling, machine-gun-toting Mexican marines, who tied up alongside while four of them boarded the inflatable. "Apparently they were on alert because some people had just been killed," says Peterson, "but finally they realized we weren't rebels and directed us to the port captain for clearance." When Peterson asked for a tow to the boat ramp, the men obligingly towed the Zodiac—"at about 10 knots, smack into the concrete ramp, which knocked a big chip out of the hull," he says. Then they tried to haul it on a tiny trailer, which immediately collapsed under its weight. *Sunrider* eventually got repaired, but the visit took over ten days and, including the charge for the damaged trailer, cost Peterson almost $1,000.

Despite the delay, Peterson, working with the Southern California Yachting Association, got some good help in finding weather windows between major storms, so *Sunrider* made it to Acapulco just behind Tropical Storm Hector and just ahead of Tropical storms Ileana and John. Then they made a few brief stops, at Puerto Vallarta, Cabo San Lucas, and Turtle Bay, along the Baja California peninsula.

Back in U.S. waters, as *Sunrider* port-hopped its way up the California coast, they finally encountered some bad weather coming around Point Conception just north of Santa Barbara. When they first hit it, Danny, who was in the cabin taking a nap, was tossed three feet up and bashed into the ceiling. "It was a bit of a roller-coaster ride, bucking 20- to 30-knot northwest winds and ten- to fifteen-foot seas," says Peterson. "But we were light on fuel, so we planed right through it, like a needle poking through a haystack." Now they were home free.

When *Sunrider* arrived in San Francisco at the end of its journey, amazingly looking none the worse for wear, it was escorted from the Golden Gate to Pier 39 by a small fleet of other soydiesel craft and a spraying fireboat. At the dock, Peterson was all smiles over the success of the Expedition. "The Zodiac was astounding—a remarkable boat beyond what I ever expected," he says. "The same goes for the equipment. I didn't expect half of it to keep working for so long in such exposed conditions—yet I had few failures in nearly 35,000 miles of travel in all the oceans of the world."

Among the large crowd on hand to greet Peterson and Danny were his wife Janice and representatives from several of the 100-plus organizations, including *Motor Boating & Sailing*, cosponsoring the venture. Peterson had succeeded in bringing his environmental message to 100 cities in forty countries, and had sparked serious inquiries from more than twenty governments interested in using soydiesel for such things as patrol boats.

His wife wasn't surprised at his success. Even at the outset, Janice had said, "My husband is not like a normal human being. Bryan has spent so much of his life as a paramedic dealing with life-and-death situations all the time that everything else—things that would have other people tearing their hair out—seems like no big deal to him." Yet his accomplishment *was* a big deal.

Peterson, in turn, says he's also proud of Danny, now fourteen, whom he saw grow into a confident young man and reliable hand during the voyage, and values the time they shared together. "We had a chance to get to know, appreciate, and enjoy each other in a wonderful way,'' he says.

Summing up the Expedition, Peterson says, ''I really loved the voyage, the many places I visited, and the friends I made in parts of the world that were only spots on the map for me two years ago. The greatest beauty has been in the hearts of the people I've met. That's what the Expedition was all about—taking our environmental message to extraordinary cultures in some of the most beautiful places on earth. And nowhere did I ever encounter a 'Yankee-go-home' attitude.''

On the other side of the coin, he says, ''For the first time, I've come to really value and appreciate what America is. We take so much for granted. I'm really struck by our freedom, including the right to say what you think. In many places you die for that. There are countries still ruled by men with guns. The lack of freedom around the world is extraordinary. In a way, the best part of the trip is coming home.''

December, 1994

⚓

COAST GUARD CAPSIZE

On a stormy night, three Coast Guardsmen die—and one sur-
vives—when their boat flips during a dramatic rescue attempt.

BY LOUISA RUDEEN

12:01 Just after midnight on February 12, a lone sailboat
struggled north along the forbidding Washington coastline
in a winter gale with 40-knot winds gusting to 50, twenty-
five-foot seas, and driving rain. It was a thirty-one-foot
fiberglass sloop of solid construction ironically called *Gale
Runner*, with a man and a woman on board, and they
weren't in real trouble—not yet.

12:15 The man, United States Navy Lieutenant Kenneth
Schlag, was sailing with his girlfriend, Marcia Infante,
from Oakland, California, to his new post on the aircraft
carrier *Carl Vinson* in Bremerton, Washington. Schlag
called the Coast Guard over the VHF; he calmly inquired
about coming into the harbor at La Push to seek refuge
from the storm. Some refuge—to get into La Push, a re-
mote outpost at the mouth of the Quillayute River, from
the south, you must first make it past a group of rock

pinnacles called the Quillayute Needles, then leave the jagged cliffs of James Island to port. Finally, in order to reach safe harbor, you must cross a river bar often boiling with angry surf.

12:26 "Mayday, Mayday, Mayday," came a weak voice from *Gale Runner* over the radio. The situation had changed drastically on the sailboat. Schlag later wrote in a brief statement: "We were exchanging information with the US Coast Guard while approaching the entrance to La Push Harbor when the boat was knocked down and rolled by a rogue wave. Hatches and portholes were blown out, leaving the boat flooding, the mast torn from the boat, and the motor flooded with water, leaving it inoperable. The boat was then left drifting without maneuverability toward the rocky shore. . . ."

This call for help immediately set into motion a chain of events that would lead to one of the worst tragedies in the history of the Coast Guard.

12:34 The forty-four-foot Motor Lifeboat (MLB) number 44363 was dispatched from Coast Guard Station Quilla-yute River in La Push. (Its motto is "Riders on the Storm.") The driver, called the "coxswain," was Petty Of-ficer Second Class David Bosley, of Coronado, California, who was thirty-six. With him were Petty Officer Third Class Matthew Schlimme of Whitewater, Missouri, who had just turned twenty-four; Seaman Clinton Miniken of Snohomish, Washington, twenty-two; and Seaman Ap-prentice Benjamin Wingo of Bremerton, nineteen. They immediately set out across the Quillayute River bar.

Standard operating procedure called for the crew to wear Mustang suits and survival vests. Each man would also buckle a safety harness around his waist with webs that could be clipped into rings mounted to "hard points" on the boat.

The 44 MLB, a steel-hulled tank with a beam of twelve feet eight inches and a draft of three feet six inches, powered by twin 185-horsepower 6V-53 Detroit Diesels, was part of a well-maintained fleet built in the 1960s for Coast Guard search-and-rescue (SAR) missions in America's worst waters. The fleet is scheduled to be replaced by new 47 MLBs—because of the 47's advanced technology and superior speed rather than any needed gain in handling or stability. Sometimes called "rollover boats," both the 44s and 47s are designed to self-right and self-bail in seconds after a knockdown or capsize. While a 360-degree rollover is certainly not a common occurrence, some 44 MLBs have gone through them. But up until this night the boats had scored a perfect record—in more than thirty years, no one had ever been lost from one.

12:45 At Coast Guard Air Station Port Angeles to the northeast, the four-man crew of HH-65 Dolphin helicopter tail number 6589 was awakened from a sound sleep in their duty berths and told to get ready to fly.

12:47 The coxswain on MLB 44363 radioed back to Station Quillayute River that they had made it across the bar, where they reported sixteen- to eighteen-foot surf and breaking seas.

12:48 One minute later, 44363 called again to report that they had capsized and were "disoriented." It was their last transmission. What happened next out there in the darkness, the slantwise rain, the howling wind, the high surf of the bar, and the heavy seas beyond is unclear; access to the one survivor's account has been restricted due to an official Coast Guard inquiry into the incident. It appears that the boat rolled over a second time. When it righted itself, Bosley and Miniken had been lost overboard.

Schlimme then took over the wheel. He turned to Wingo and made sure he was "properly buckled in."

Then the boat capsized for the third time. When it came back up, Wingo was alone.

12:49   "Mayday, Mayday, this is the sailing vessel *Gale Runner*," the Coast Guard station's radio crackled again. Presumably reading off his GPS, Schlag gave his position as 47 degrees, 51.9 minutes north, 124 degrees, 39.2 minutes west.

12:58   The crew of a second MLB, 44393, got under way from Station Quillayute River.

1:10   The second lifeboat reported that they were across the bar, but had lost a radio antenna in transit. They began to search for the first MLB. At some point they saw flares go up, possibly shot off by Wingo, who would have had a flare kit in his survival vest, but in the midst of the storm the crew on 44393 had difficulty locating their source.

1:18   The Dolphin helicopter took off from Air Station Port Angeles. By coincidence, both the pilot and copilot, Commander Paul Langlois and Commander Ray Miller, were senior, decorated airmen. There is always a moment of radio silence on liftoff. When communications were reestablished, they learned that Station Quillayute River had "lost coms" (communications) with MLB 44363, and their own guys might be missing. "Our focus shifted," said Langlois. He flew west down the Straits of Juan de Fuca, then made a 90-degree turn around Cape Flattery, rather than fly a more direct route over the Olympic Mountains and risk heavy turbulence.

1:57   The Dolphin arrived at the Quillayute River bar. Instead of heading for *Gale Runner* a little farther to the south, the helicopter crew began searching for MLB 44363. Miller was using special ITT night vision equipment. "Ray has more experience on night vision goggles than most pilots in the Coast Guard," Langlois said. In the black night, with no moon or stars and only ambient light from tiny La Push, visibility ranged from a half mile to two miles.

2:03   Station Quillayute River called the Dolphin and asked it to divert to the crippled sailboat, which was being driven by wind and sea toward the Needles rock formation. The pilots heard the voice of the station's Officer in Charge, Master Chief George LaForge, say, "You better go get them, because they're not going to stand a chance if you don't."

2:05   Miller had the sailboat's position on his radar screen. Langlois flew to it and attempted to drop down beside it with his nose in the wind. After one abortive attempt, he finally managed to hover beside *Gale Runner*, which they could now see. A single light shone from its cabin as it was tossed around by twenty-five-foot waves.

With no visual reference in front of him, Langlois found it tough to maintain the hover, hanging anywhere from twenty-five to seventy-five feet above the surface depending on whether they were over a wave crest or trough. And they had a bigger problem: Looking aft,

Miller could see the Needles, some of the rocks thrusting up over 150 feet, only 300 yards behind them.

"As each passing minute went by, we were drifting backward in formation with the sailboat," Langlois said. He had already briefed Schlag and Infante over the radio about the helicopter hoist. "We thought we had to do it as quickly as we could," the pilot said. The Dolphin's flight mechanic, Petty Officer Third Class Neal Amos, tried to lower the rescue basket on its long cable to Gale Runner's deck. Miller later likened it to trying to position an object "about the size of a large executive office chair" onto a space "about the size of a large executive office desk," when both are moving wildly back and forth. " 'Wild' would be an understatement," he said.

2:30   When boat and helicopter were only seventy-five yards off the Needles, Langlois was forced to abort the attempt and pull up. "It was very difficult for us to stop," he said.

The sailboat was now in even bigger seas reflecting off the stone pillars. "I could see with my night vision goggles that they were headed toward a shelf of rock—a very solid shelf with waves crashing on it," Miller said. "I told them to get below and brace themselves." First, Gale Runner was pushed through a narrow space between two spires. "Just before they hit, they actually threaded the needle," he said. Then the sailboat smashed onto the rock ledge and lay there, on its side, ten feet up in the air. "I thought there's no way they're going to be able to survive this," Miller said.

"The next breaker washed them off the shelf," Langlois said. Incredibly, the boat popped upright and the people on board were still alive.

Now *Gale Runner* was in an area where the waves were dampened by the line of rocks, and the helicopter was able to set up for a successful hoist. When Amos got the basket to the deck, Infante jumped in just before a wave snatched it away. It swung like a pendulum on the way up, but she made it to the chopper unharmed. Then the flight mechanic sent the basket back down for Schlag. Once they had him safely on board, "We immediately got the heck out of there," Langlois said.

2:42 Long-range HH-60 Jayhawk helicopter tail number 6003 arrived on the scene from Air Station Astoria in Oregon, 110 miles to the south. The pilot, Commander Mike Neussl, was asked by Station Quillayute River to stay clear until the Dolphin had completed its rescue. Below, he could see the second MLB "taking a pounding" while it searched for the missing men.

As the Jayhawk flew out past James Island, the flight mechanic, Rick Vanlandingham, thought he saw a red flare go up. But since he'd heard the other air crew radio a request that flares be lit to mark a ballfield near the Coast Guard station—also in his line of sight—he thought that's what he was looking at.

2:50 Langlois set the Dolphin down on the ballfield, and Schlag and Infante were transferred to a waiting ambulance. They were driven upriver to Forks Community Hospital, where they were treated for bruises, cuts, and hypothermia, and released.

In the statement, Schlag wrote: "We would like to express our gratitude to . . . the U.S. Coast Guard, particularly those who risked their lives during the rescue operation. We would further like to express our deepest sorrow to the families and friends of the men who lost their lives while saving ours." Citing that he was cooperating with the inquiry board, he declined requests to speak to the media.

"The fact that we were able to save those two lives was very gratifying," Miller said. "It has kept me going throughout the aftermath—the loss of our own crew."

2:51   "For lack of a better term, we were getting the crap knocked out of us," Neussl said of the turbulence in the lee of James Island. The Jayhawk team was now searching for the missing MLB with sophisticated SAR technology. The pilots wore night vision goggles. In the back, Petty Officer Second Class James Lyon operated the Forward-Looking Infrared (FLIR) equipment, hoping to find a survivor by picking up his body heat on the sensor. Vanlandingham was on the Night Sun searchlight, which puts out six million candlepower in a focused beam.

3:10   Neussl began to fly an oval "racetrack" search pattern. "We were looking for anything that didn't look like white crashing surf and rocks," he said. They had two false alarms. The first was the wreck of the *Gale Runner*, now lying with a broken keel on Second Beach south of town. The other was a white warning ball on the power lines running from the mainland out to James Island. "We broke off that approach quickly," Neussl said.

3:30   Nearly the entire population of La Push, along with about 100 members of the local Quileute Native American tribe, which has close ties to the Coast Guard station, had turned out to search the shoreline, shouting to each other above the wind. Miniken's body was found where it had washed up on First Beach. He was given CPR in a futile attempt to revive him, and was pronounced dead at the

Forks hospital. Miniken had been in the Coast Guard for eight months.

3:48 Looking across the Jayhawk's cockpit, Lieutenant Todd Trimpert, the copilot, saw a flashing light on James Island. He told Neussl, who positioned the helicopter above a narrow cove on the island's western side. The mouth of the cove was foaming with surf; inside, a thin wedge of rocky beach strewn with timber lay between towering cliffs over 200 feet high. Part way up one of the cliffs, in the rocks, they spotted what looked like a strobe light. When they aimed the Night Sun searchlight at it, they also saw a flash of reflective material. "And we saw the hull of the boat," Neussl said. He couldn't believe that the MLB had gotten in there. "Everything must have had to line up just right. It was a tight fit. I don't think you could fit a 44-footer crossways into that cove," he said. MLB 44363 was sitting upright, and its motors had still been running when it hit the beach—the inquiry board later found chewed-up rocks indicating that the props had been spinning. "It did what it was designed to do," said Captain Carmond Fitzgerald, the board's senior officer.

At first, the Jayhawk crew members were unable to confirm that they had actually found a person; they were afraid the strobe was on an empty survival vest flung up there by the surf. The FLIR didn't sense any body heat (as it turned out, Wingo had done too good a job of insulating himself against the elements by putting up his hood). So Neussl dropped down for a better look. Then they were pretty sure they had a survivor, but the turbulence was too severe for them to land. "I decided that I wasn't going to put the aircraft down in that cove, because I didn't think it was going to come back out," he said. A hoist was also out of the question. Neussl called the station and recommended that a "high-angle" cliff rescue team be dispatched to the scene.

4:00   The Jayhawk assumed a hover above the cove, which it held for more than two hours, shining its big light down. "The most important thing in surviving an incident like this one is the will to live," Neussl said. "We felt we were providing the will to live for the guy hanging on the cliff."

Sadly, the Night Sun searchlight also picked up the flash of reflective tape on backs of the Mustang suits worn by two bodies lying facedown in the water of the cove. One was Bosley, a decorated veteran of eleven years, who was to be transferred home to California that summer. The other, Schlimme, had been due to leave the Coast Guard in just over a fortnight.

6:20   Finally low on fuel, the first Jayhawk did a direct "handoff" to a second HH-60 out of Astoria, tail number 6013, piloted by Lieutenant Timothy Heitch, who took up Neussl's position.

6:45   Word came over the second Jayhawk's radio that the Clallam County Sheriff's Department cliff rescue team had come down from Port Angeles and was assembling at Station Quillayute River. In the helicopter, Petty Officer First Class Tom Smylie, who had high-angle rescue training himself, volunteered to evaluate the terrain for the team. Heitch flew up over the cliff and found a slightly less inhospitable part of the island. But due to the still-high winds, the crew had to lower Smylie down to it in the basket from over 150 feet up. "I was buffeted around a lot," he said. Once on the ground, "I looked over the cliff and saw an arm waving a light," Smylie said. When he radioed this back to the helicopter, "It got everybody really excited." He scrambled down as far as he could safely go without equipment, but stopped short at a 100-foot sheer vertical face. Wingo was at its base. A recent high school star athlete in soccer and basketball, he had jumped off the MLB when it hit the beach and climbed up the cliff as far as he could get. Smylie called down to ask how he was and reported, "He said he was okay."

7:00 The sky finally began to lighten. "Once daylight breaks, that gives you a lot of perspective on things," Heitch said. He and his crew brought the volunteer rescue team over from the mainland and hoisted it down to the island. With Smylie helping to coordinate from the top, the team rappeled on ropes down the steep cliff to Wingo.

8:14 The survivor was hoisted into the Jayhawk and flown to the station. He had suffered only a broken nose and facial lacerations. Wingo had been with the Coast Guard for four months.

After eight hours, the nightmare was over. Three people were dead, but thanks largely to the training, talent, heroism and tenacity of the U.S. Coast Guard, three people had survived.

Bosley, Miniken, and Schlimme were honored in La Push by a memorial service and a traditional blanket-giving ceremony held by the Quileute Tribe. Wingo was later awarded the Coast Guard Medal for extraordinary heroism.

Whatever the final analysis of this tragedy, there's a lesson here for all boaters: Stay on top of marine weather forecasts, and if it's going to be bad out there, don't let time pressures, peers, or an exaggerated faith in your own abilities make you put to sea. You can always wait it out in port. Because, if you get into trouble, the Coast Guard will come for you with everything its got. And then you'll be putting many more lives at risk than just your own.

May, 1997

About the Authors

Roy Attaway worked for *Motor Boating & Sailing* in the late seventies, and returned to the staff as a senior editor and photographer in 1997.

Craig Barrie, a longtime offshore racer, is president of high performance boat manufacturer Cigarette Racing Team.

John Clemans is an *MB&S* senior editor. He often crosses the Gulf Stream from his Florida home to the Bahamas— on his twenty-two-foot inflatable.

Shearlean Duke has contributed several stories to *MB&S*. A former *L. A. Times* editor, she teaches journalism at a North Carolina university.

Joane Fishman is a former *MB&S* contributing editor. She has also served as the yachting correspondent for *The New York Times*.

Hank Halsted is a former *MB&S* contributing editor who now runs a yacht brokerage in Newport, Rhode Island.

Peter A. Janssen is editor-in-chief and publisher of *MB&S*. Lately, he has driven a Fountain power catamaran to a speed of 162 miles per hour.

Dag Pike is a British author and adventurer who's set many boating records—including a powerboat transatlantic crossing record with Richard Branson.

Louisa Rudeen is managing editor of *MB&S*. One of her wildest rides was punching through big surf on a U.S. Coast Guard rollover lifeboat.

Sid Stapleton is an *MB&S* contributing editor. He made an epic, 15,000-mile cruise of the Americas at the helm of Grand Banks 49 *Americas Odyssey*.

Ted Turner is a cable television magnate and sailboat racer who won the America's Cup on *Courageous* in 1977.

Michael Verdon is a former *MB&S* senior editor. He has lived and boated all over the world, including Ireland and the Virgin Islands.

Polly Whittell is an *MB&S* senior editor. She has interviewed many celebrity boat owners, and many of boating's most celebrated record-holders.

Bonnie Waitzken has contributed several stories to *MB&S*. She currently teaches chess in New York City schools. Her son is *Searching for Bobby Fischer* chess prodigy Josh Waitzken.

Peter Wright is an *MB&S* Contributing Editor and sportfishing captain who has caught more 1,000-pound black marlin than any other man alive.

Permissions

"Across the Atlantic by Outboard" published as "Across the Atlantic by Outboard—a First" by Al Grover as told to Polly Whittell, December, 1985. Copyright © 1985 by Polly Whittell.

"Adrift in the South Pacific" by Shearlean Duke, published as "How a Family Survived 24 Days Adrift in the South Pacific," April, 1983. Copyright © 1983 by Shearlean Duke.

"The Agony of Andrew," also titled "Andrew," by Michael Verdon, November, 1992. Copyright © 1992 by Michael Verdon.

"American Hero" by Polly Whittell, published as "American Hero: Dodge Morgan," July, 1986, and "Around the World Alone–Nonstop," January, 1986. Copyright © 1986 by Polly Whittell.

"Blood, Sweat & Tears" by Louisa Rudeen, June, 1988. Copyright © 1988 by Louisa E. Rudeen.